ISBN 978-1-330-97401-8
PIBN 10128387

HE SATIRES OF DRYDEN.

MACMILLAN AND CO., Limited
LONDON · BOMBAY · CALCUTTA
MELBOURNE

THE MACMILLAN COMPANY
NEW YORK · BOSTON · CHICAGO
ATLANTA · SAN FRANCISCO

THE MACMILLAN CO. OF CANADA, Ltd.
TORONTO

atires of Dryden

Absalom and Achitophel
The Medal, Mac Flecknoe

EDITED WITH MEMOIR, INTRODUCTION,
AND NOTES BY

John Churton Collins

MACMILLAN AND CO., LIMITED
ST. MARTIN'S STREET, LONDON

1909

First Edition 1897.
Reprinted 1903, 1905, 1909.

GLASGOW : PRINTED AT THE UNIVERSI
BY ROBERT MACLEHOSE AND CO.

PREFACE.

A GRATEFUL confession of immense indebtedness to
the labours of Sir Walter Scott and Mr. W. D. Christie
is, and always must be, incumbent on any Editor of
the Satires of Dryden. My own indebtedness to them
is too great to be specified in detail, and I must therefore satisfy myself with this general acknowledgment.
But if they did much they have also left much to be
done. Those who have made Dryden a subject of
special study will see that I have contributed something, in addition to what I have derived from those
excellent commentators, towards the elucidation of
obscure passages, and something also in the way of
new illustrations and parallels. With two or three
deviations Mr. Christie's text is adopted throughout,
and as this edition is designed rather for students of
literature and students of history than for those who
are interested in textual criticism, I have not thought
it necessary either to discuss or mark various readings.
Dryden is not a classic in whose style minutiæ of
this kind are of importance.

The notes on the Second Part of *Absalom and
Achitophel* have been designedly curtailed; it would

be absurd to suppose that the rubbish of Tate would find critical readers now, but as Tate's contribution is interesting historically it has been reprinted in its entirety, and the historical references have been explained.

To prevent possible misunderstanding I ought perhaps to add, that in the Memoir and General Introduction I have incorporated, here and there, a few sentences from an article on Dryden contributed by me some years ago to the *Quarterly Review*.

CONTENTS.

MEMOIR OF DRYDEN.

JOHN DRYDEN, one of the most distinguished among poets of the secondary rank, the founder of an important dynasty of English poets, and the father of English criticism, was born at Aldwincle, a village near Oundle in Northamptonshire, on the 9th of August, 1631. His family, though not noble, was eminently respectable. His paternal grandfather, Sir Erasmus Dryden, was a baronet, and through his mother, Mary Pickering, he was at once the great-grandson of one baronet, Sir Gilbert Pickering, and the first cousin of Sir Gilbert's namesake and immediate successor. In the great revolution of the 17th century both the Drydens and the Pickerings were on the side of the Parliament. And when, many years afterwards, Dryden became the champion of the Court Party and the Roman Catholics, he was reminded, with taunts, that one of his uncles had turned the chancel of the church at Canons Ashbey into a barn, and that his father had served as a Committee man.

Of his early youth little is known. If the inscription on the monument erected by his cousin, Mrs. Creed, in Tichmarsh Church be trustworthy, he received the rudiments of his education some-

where in that village. From Tichmarsh he passed
to Westminster School, probably about 1642. We
have now no means of knowing the exact date of his
entering Westminster, nor do we know why this
particular school was selected. But the choice was a
wise one. Richard Busby had, some three years
before, succeeded Osbolston in the headmastership.
Under Osbolston the school had greatly declined, but
it was now, in Busby's hands, rapidly rising to the
first place among English schools of that day, and
Dryden had the inestimable advantage of being the
pupil of a man who was destined to become the king
of English schoolmasters. "I have known great numbers of his scholars," writes Steele, "and am confident
I could discover a stranger who had been such with
a very little conversation. Those of great parts who
have passed through his instruction have such a peculiar
readiness of fancy and delicacy of taste as is seldom
found in men educated elsewhere, though of equal
talents." Among Busby's pupils were the poets Lee,
Prior, King, Rowe, Duke, and the learned Edmund
Smith, the philosopher Locke, the theologians South
and Atterbury, the most illustrious of English financiers,
Charles Montagu, afterwards Earl of Halifax; the poet-
diplomatist, George Stepney; the most accomplished
of physicians, John Friend; the wits and scholars,
Robert Friend and Anthony Alsop; the distinguished
classical scholar, Mattaire; while he could boast that
eight of his pupils had been raised to the bench, and
that no less than sixteen had become bishops. Busby's
influence on Dryden was undoubtedly great. He saw
and encouraged his peculiar bent. He appears to have

allowed him to substitute composition in English for composition in Latin and Greek, and he encouraged him to turn portions of Persius and other Roman poets into English verse. Despairing, probably, of ever making him an exact verbal scholar, he was satisfied with enabling him to read Latin, if not Greek, with accuracy and facility. Dryden never forgot his obligations to Busby. Thirty years afterwards, when the Westminster boy had become the first poet and the first critic of his age, he dedicated, with exquisite propriety, to his old schoolmaster his translation of the Satire in which Persius records his reverence and gratitude to Cornutus. From Westminster he proceeded to Trinity College, Cambridge. He was entered on the 18th of May, 1650; he matriculated in the following July, and on the 2nd of October in the same year he was elected a scholar on the Westminster foundation. Of his life at Cambridge very little is known. Like Milton before him, and like Gray, Wordsworth, and Coleridge after him, he appears to have had no respect for his teachers, and to have taken his education into his own hands. From independence to rebellion is an easy step, and an entry may still be read in the Conclusion-book at Trinity, which charges him with disobedience to the Vice-Master and with contumacy in taking the punishment inflicted on him. It would seem also from an allusion in a satire of Shadwell's that he got into some scrape for libelling a young nobleman, which, had he not anticipated condemnation by flight, would have ended in his expulsion from the University. But as this is without corroboration of any kind and rests only on the authority of

Shadwell, it is now impossible to disengage the little
which is probably true in the story from the greater
part which is plainly fictitious.   How long Dryden
remained at Cambridge is uncertain.   He took the
degree of B.A. in January, 1654.   In June of the
same year his father died, and on his father's death
he succeeded to a small property.   Of his movements
during the next three years nothing certain is known.
It seems clear that he did not return, as Malone and
the biographers who have followed Malone have supposed, to Cambridge.   By the middle of 1657 he had in
all probability settled in London.

Cromwell was then, though harassed with accumulat-
ing difficulties, in the zenith of his power, and Dryden's
cousin, Sir Gilbert Pickering, stood high in the Protector's favour.   As young Dryden was on friendly terms
with Sir Gilbert, who appears to have received him with
much kindness, he had good reason for supposing that
an opening would soon be found for him.   His social
and political prospects were indeed far more promising
than his prospects as a poet.   He was now in his twenty-
seventh year.   At an age when Aristophanes, Catullus,
Lucan, Persius, Milton, Tasso, Shelley, Keats, and innumerable others, had won immortal fame, he had evinced
no symptom of poetic genius; he had proved, on the
contrary, that he was ignorant of the very rudiments of
his art, that he had still to acquire what all other poets
instinctively possess.   A few lines to his cousin, Honor,
"so middling bad were better," an execrable elegy on
Lord Hasting's death, and a commendatory poem on his
friend Hoddesden's Epigrams immeasurably inferior to
what Pope and Kirke White produced at twelve, showed

that he had no ear for verse, no command of poetic diction, no sense of poetic taste. The transformation of the author of these poems into the author of *Absalom and Achitophel*, the *Religio Laici*, and the *Hind and Panther*, is one of the most remarkable in the history of literature.

Sir Gilbert was not able to do much for his young relative. 'In September, 1658, Cromwell died, and at the beginning of the following year Dryden published a copy of verses to deplore the event. The *Heroic Stanzas on the Death of the Lord Protector* inaugurate his poetical career. His biography from this point may be conveniently divided into four epochs. The first extends to the publication of the *Essay of Dramatic Poesy* in 1668, the second to the appearance of the *Spanish Friar* in the autumn of 1681, the third to the publication of the *Britannia Rediviva* in June, 1688, and the fourth to his death in 1700.

1659-1668.

The death of Cromwell changed the face of affairs, and, after nearly eighteen months of anarchy, Charles II. was on the throne of his ancestors. Dryden lost no time in attempting to ingratiate himself with the Royalists, and the three poems succeeding the *Heroic Stanzas*, namely, *Astræa Redux* (1660), the *Panegyric on the Coronation* (April, 1661), and the *Epistle to the Lord Chancellor* (New Year's Day, 1662), were written to welcome Charles II. and to flatter his minister Clarendon. These poems are evidently the fruit of much labour, and recall in their versification and tone of thought the characteristics of the masters of the "Critical School"—

Waller, Denham, Cowley, and Davenant, plainly Dryden's models at this time.   In November, 1662, Dryden
became a member of the newly-founded Royal Society,
and in the following year his interest in scientific
studies found expression in a copy of verses addressed
to Dr. Walter Charleton, and inserted in Charleton's
treatise on Stonehenge.   This, according to Hallam, is
the first of Dryden's poems which "possesses any considerable merit," the first, as Scott observes, in which he
threw off the shackles of the "Metaphysical School," as
it is certainly the first in which he strikes his own
peculiar note.

Dryden had now seriously commenced his career
as a professional man of letters, and attached himself
to Herringman, a bookseller in the New Exchange.
For some months he appears to have been a kind
of hack to Herringman, producing various trifles in
current ephemeral publications.   In 1663, he took
two important steps, which were to affect greatly his
future life.   In December he married the Lady Elizabeth Howard, the sister of his friend Sir Robert
Howard, and one of the daughters of the Earl of
Berkshire.   She bore him three sons, but it does
not appear to have been a happy marriage, and
though we need not suppose that Dryden's frequent
and bitter sneers at marriage were anything more
than a concession to the fashionable cant of the age,
it is not unlikely that his own experience, in some
degree, flavoured and coloured them.   Shortly before
his marriage, began his connection with the theatres,
and this connection was, with some interruptions, continued till within six years of his death, his first play,

The Wild Gallant, being acted in 1663, his last, *Love Triumphant*, in 1694. Johnson has lamented the necessity of following the progress of Dryden's theatrical fame, but observes at the same time that the composition and fate of eight and twenty dramas include too much of a poetical life to be omitted. They include, unhappily, the best years of that life ; they prevented, as their author pathetically complains, the composition of works better suited to his genius. Had fortune allowed him to indulge that genius Lucretius might have found his equal and Lucan his superior. He had bound himself, however, to the profession of a man of letters ; he had taken to literature as a trade, and it was, therefore, necessary for him to supply not the commodities of which he happened to have a monopoly, but the commodities of which his customers had need. Those who live to please must, as he well knew, please to live. His first play, *The Wild Gallant* (1663), was a failure. "As poor a thing," writes Pepys, "as ever as I saw in my life." Comedy, indeed, as he soon found, was not within his range, and though he lived to produce five others by dint of wholesale plagiarism from Molière, Quinault, Corneille, and Plautus, and by laboriously interpolating indecency which may challenge comparison with Lindsay's *Philotus* or Fletcher's *Custom of the County*, two of them were hissed off the stage, one was indifferently received, and the other two are inferior in comic effect to the poorest of Wycherley's. He says himself in the *Defence of the Essay on Dramatic Poesy*, "I am not so fitted by nature to write comedy. I want that gaiety of humour which is required to it. My conversation is slow and

b

dull, my humour saturnine and reserved. So that those
who decry my comedies do me no injury except it be in
point of profit; reputation in them is the last thing
to which I shall pretend." He had indeed no humour;
he had no grace; he had no eye for those finer impro-
prieties of character and conduct which are to comedy
what passion is to tragedy. What wit he had was
coarse and serious; he had no power of inventing
ludicrous incidents; he could not manage the light
artillery of colloquial raillery. In his next play, *The
Rival Ladies* (printed in 1664), he exchanged in the
lighter parts plain prose for blank verse, and he wrote
the tragic portions in highly elaborate rhyming couplets,
prefixing to it, in the form of a dedicatory Epistle to the
Earl of Orrery, the first of those delightful critical prefaces which form one of the most valuable and pleasing
portions of his writings. *The Rival Ladies* was well received, and he hastened to assist his friend and brother-
in-law, Sir Robert Howard, in the composition of *The
Indian Queen* (January, 1664). This was a great success.
It probably revealed to Dryden where his real strength
lay. The drama belonged to those curious exotics
known as the Heroic Plays. Of these plays, of their
origin and character, Dryden has himself given us an
interesting account in the essay prefixed to *The Conquest
of Granada.*

"The first light we had of them in the English Theatre was
from the late Sir William Davenant. It being forbidden him in
the rebellious times to act tragedies and comedies, because they
contained some matter of scandal to those good people who could
more easily dispossess their lawful sovereign than endure a
wanton jest, he was forced to turn his thoughts another way,
and to introduce the examples of moral virtue, writ in verse, and

performed in recitative music. The original of this music he had from the Italian operas; but he heightened his characters (as I may probably imagine) from the example of Corneille and some French poets. In this condition did this part of poetry remain at his Majesty's return, when growing bolder, as being now owned by a public authority, he reviewed his *Siege of Rhodes*, and caused it to be acted as a just drama. For myself and others who came after him we are bound, with all veneration to his memory, to acknowledge what advantage we received from that excellent ground work which he laid. . . Having done him this justice as my guide, I will do myself so much as to give an account of what I have performed after him. I observed then, as I said, what was wanting to the perfection of his *Siege of Rhodes*, which was design and variety of characters. And in the midst of this consideration, by mere accident, I opened the next book that lay by me, which was an Ariosto in Italian; and the very first two lines of that poem gave me light to all I could desire—

    ' Le donne, i cavalier, l'arme, gli amori,
    Le cortesie, l'audaci imprese io canto.'

For the very next reflection that I made was this: that an heroic play ought to be an imitation in little of an heroic poem, and consequently that love and valour ought to be the subject of it."*

Dryden has omitted to notice that these plays undoubtedly owed much both to the French dramatists, particularly to Corneille, and to the French Heroic Romances of D'Urfé, Gomberville, Calprenède, and

* Dr. Ward, following Sir Walter Scott and others, asserts in his *English Dramatic Literature* that Roger Boyle, Earl of Orrery, was the originator of these rhymed Heroic Plays, and he refers in proof of the statement to Dryden's Preface to *The Rival Ladies*. But Dryden says nothing of the kind. He represents himself as being the originator of these plays, afterwards modifying this statement by assigning to Davenant the credit of having given the hint for them.

Madame de Scuderi, borrowing from the first the cast
of the rhymed verse, and from the second the stilted
and bombastic sentiment, as well as innumerable hints
in matters of detail.

With this notion of the scope and functions of the
Heroic Drama, Dryden set to work. Carefully selecting
such material as would be most appropriate for rhetorical
treatment and most remote from ordinary life, he drew
sometimes on the Heroic French Romances, as in *The
Maiden Queen*, which is derived from *The Grand Cyrus*,
and in *The Conquest of Granada*, which is based on the
Almahide of Madame Scuderi; sometimes on the exotic
fictions of Spanish, Portuguese, or Eastern legend, as in
The Indian Emperor and *Aurengzebe;* or on the misty
annals of early Christian martyrology, as in *The Royal
Martyr;* or on the dreamland of poets, as in *The State of
Innocence*. All is false and unreal. The world in which
his characters move is not merely a world which has no
counterpart in human experience, but is so incongruous
and chaotic that it is simply unintelligible and unim-
aginable, even as fiction. His men and women are men
and women on*l*y by courtesy. It would be more correct
to speak of them as puppets tricked out in phantastic
tinsel, the showman, as he jerks them, not taking the
trouble to speak through them in falsetto, but merely talking in his natural voice. And in nearly every drama we
have the same leading puppets—the one in a male, the
other in a female form. The male impersonates either a
ranting, blustering tyrant, all fanfarado and bombast,
like Almanzor and Maximim, or some sorely-tried and
pseudo-chivalrous hero, like Cortez and Aurungzebe; the
female some meretricious Dulcinea, who is the object of

the male hero's desires and adoration. This Dulcinea
has usually some rival Dulcinea to vex and bring her
out, and the tyrant, or *preux chevalier*, some rival
opponent who serves the same purpose. This enables
the poet to pit these characters against each other in
declamation and dialogue, and it is these interbanded
declamations and dialogues which make up the greater
part, or at least the most effective parts, of the dramas.
Not that scenic effects are ignored, for battles, processions, feasts, sensational arrests, harryings, murders,
and attempted murders, outrages, and every variety of
agitating surprise break up and diversify these dialogues
and declamations with most admired disorder. But
worthless and absurd as these plays are from a dramatic
point of view, they are very far from being without merit.
The charm of their versification, which is seen in its
highest perfection in *The Conquest of Granada*, *The Indian
Emperor*, *Aurengzebe*, and *The State of Innocence* is irre-
sistible, preserving a singular and exquisite combination
of dignity and grace, of vigour and sweetness. Dryden
is always impressive when he clothes moral reflections
in verse, and some of his finest passages in this kind are
to be found in these plays. But perhaps their most
remarkable feature is the rhymed argumentative dialogue.
Dryden's power of maintaining an argument in verse,
of putting with epigrammatic terseness, in sonorous and musical rhythm, the case for and against
in any given subject, was unrivalled; and he
revelled in its exercise. We may select for illustration the dialogue between Almanzor and Almahide in the third act of the *First Part of the Conquest of Granada;* that between Cydaria and Cortez in

the second act of *The Conquest of Mexico;* that between Indamora and Arimant in the second act of *Aurengzebe;* and that in which St. Catharine converts Apollonius from Paganism to Christianity in the second act of *Tyrannic Love.* But if these plays add nothing to Dryden's reputation, it was in their composition that he trained, developed, and matured the powers which enabled him to produce with a rapidity so wonderful the masterpieces on which his fame rests.

In the summer of 1665 the plague closed the theatres, and drove all whose circumstances enabled them to leave London into the country. The greater part of the time intervening between the breaking up of the plague and the beginning of 1667 Dryden appears to have passed at Charlton Park, in Wiltshire, the seat of his father-in-law. He occupied his time in the production of two memorable works—the *Annus Mirabilis* and the *Essay of Dramatic Poesy*—the one being published in 1667, the other in 1668.* Both these works may be said to mark epochs in the history of English literature. The *Annus Mirabilis,* which is a historical narrative of the chief incidents of the year 1666—the war against Holland in coalition with France, and the Fire of London—exhibits with singular precision the characteristics of that school of poetry of which Dryden was to be the leader—the poetry of rhetoric. In the *Essay of Dramatic Poesy* Dryden not only gave the first striking illustration of his characteristic prose style, but he produced what is incom-

---

* It was entered on the Stationers' Books August 7th, 1667, and, according to Malone, published in that year, but the date on the title page of the first edition is 1668 : books, it may be added, were in those days not unfrequently ante-dated.

parably the (best critical treatise)which had appeared in our language. From the *Annus Mirabilis* dates the defin ition and dominance of the " Critical School " in poetry ; from the *Essay of Dramatic Poesy* the definition and domin- ance of the modern as distinguished from the Elizabethan and Caroline style, and the appearance in England of literary criticism in the modern sense of the term.

1668–1681.

On his return to London, probably in the autumn of 1667, he betook himself immediately to dramatic work, and about this time contracted with the Company of the King's Theatre to supply them, in consideration of receiving a share and a quarter of the profits of the theatre, with three plays a year. He did not fulfil his share of the contract, but the Company, with great liberality, allowed him to receive, in return for the plays which he did write, the full sum originally agreed upon. It is not necessary to enumerate the plays produced by him during these years. In August, 1670, he succeeded James Howell as Historiographer Royal, and Sir William Davenant as Poet Laureate.

And now he was brought into contact with opponents who disturbed his peace, and whom he was destined to gibbet, for the amusement of contemporaries and posterity,—with Zimri and Doeg, with Og and Mephi- bosheth. Dryden's Heroic Plays were at this time the rage of the town. How easily they lent themselves to ridicule, to ludicrous parodies of their style, to burlesque travesties of their sentiments, their incidents and their characters, must have been obvious to any mischievous humourist. The Duke of Buckingham, then one of the

leading wits and most prominent figures in Court and in
theatrical circles, had long had his eye on them. Calling
to his assistance Martin Clifford, Thomas Sprat, and, it
is said, Samuel Butler, he produced a farce called *The
Rehearsal*—a farce which subsequently furnished Sheridan
with the idea and with many of the points of *The Critic*.
The central figure of the piece is a silly and conceited
dramatist, Bayes; and Bayes is Dryden. With all the
licence of the Athenian stage, Dryden's personal peculi-
arities, his florid complexion, his dress, his snuff-taking,
the tone of his voice, his gestures, his favourite oaths,
"Gad's my life," "I'fackins," "Gadsooks," and the
like, were faithfully caught and copied. Buckingham,
who was inimitable as a mimic, spent immense pains in
training Lacy, the actor, to sustain the part. In a few
weeks Bayes, indistinguishable from Dryden, was con-
vulsing all London with laughter, and Dryden had moreover the mortification of hearing that the very theatre,
which had, a few nights before, been ringing with the
sonorous couplets of his *Siege of Granada*, was now hoarse
with laughing at ludicrous parodies of his favourite
passages and most effective scenes. He made no immediate reply, but calmly, or with affected indifference,
admitted that the satire had a great many good strokes.
But this was not the only annoyance to which he was
submitted. About a year and a half afterwards Wilmot,
Earl of Rochester, had for some reason, which cannot
now be certainly explained, resolved to annoy Dryden.
He had for this purpose become the patron of a wretched
poetaster named Elkanah Settle, who had just written a
play in every way worthy of its author, entitled *The
Empress of Morocco*. By the Earl's influence it was acted

at Whitehall, the lords at Court and the maids of honour supporting the principal characters. It was then splendidly printed, adorned with cuts, and inscribed to the Earl of Norwich in a dedication in which Dryden was studiously insulted. The town was loud in its praises, and Dryden, it was said, had found a formidable rival.

With *Aurengzebe*, which appeared in 1675, Dryden closed his series of Heroic Plays. He had now, he said, another taste of wit, and was growing weary of his long-loved mistress, Rhyme. "He was anxious indeed," as he writes in the interesting dedication of *Aurengzebe* to Mulgrave, "to make the world amends for many ill plays by an heroic poem," and this project he long nursed. In his *Essay on Satire* he tells that he had had two subjects for such a poem in his mind—the one King Arthur conquering the Saxons, the other the subjugation of Spain and the restoration of Pedro by the Black Prince. But poverty compelled him to abandon the idea, and the necessity of providing for the passing hour confined him to deal only with what was of interest to the passing hour, and to the passing hour, unhappily, of the world of Charles II. And so it was left for Scott to lament—

> " Dryden in immortal strain
> Had rais'd the Table Round again,
> But that a ribbald King and Court
> Bade him toil on to make them sport,
> Demanded for their niggard pay,
> Fit for their souls a looser lay,
> Licentious satire, song and play.
> The world defrauded of the high design
> Profaned the God-given strength and marr'd the
> lofty rhyme." *

* Introduction to Marmion.

Macaulay, though fully aware of the limitations of Dryden's powers as a poet, regrets that this heroic poem was never written. But the loss is probably not a great one. Nature never intended him to be the rival of Virgil and Milton, but there is every indication that she had well qualified him to become the rival of Lucretius and Juvenal.

In his next play, *All for Love* (1677–8), he declared himself the disciple of Shakespeare, and exchanged rhyme for blank verse. It stands with *Don Sebastian* at the head of his dramas, and may be said to stand high in tragedy of the secondary order—of the tragedy, that is to say, of rhetoric, as distinguished from the tragedy of nature and passion. Dryden was now at the height of his theatrical fame. *All for Love* had been a great success, and though the plays produced subsequently— *Œdipus* written in conjunction with Nathaniel Lee, *Troilus and Cressida*, and *Limberham,* the most disgraceful of his comedies—had not maintained his reputation, in *The Spanish Friar* he struck a note which found response enthusiastic, even to frenzy, in the breasts of thousands. It appeared in the autumn of 1681. The nation was now on fire with faction, and a momentous crisis in the struggle between the Court Party and the Roman Catholics on the one hand, and the County Party and Exclusionists on the other, was at hand. *The Spanish Friar*, a virulent attack on the Roman Catholics and the Anti-Exclusionists, was the first of Dryden's contributions to the great religious and political controversy of the time. It marks the transition from the second to the third epoch into which we have divided his career.

1681–1688.

During these years Dryden produced his most important poems, three of which, the satires *Absalom and Achitophel*, *The Medal*, and *Mac Flecknoe* are printed with introductions and notes in this volume. In these introductions and notes will, I hope, be found all that is required to elucidate the political and literary controversies in which Dryden was, during this period, engaged. It will only, therefore, be necessary here to say a few words about the other works which employed him. The first part of *Absalom and Achitophel* appeared in November, 1681; *The Medal* in the beginning of March, 1682; *Mac Flecknoe* in October, and the second part of *Absalom and Achitophel* in the following November. Simultaneously with the last poem was published the *Religio Laici*. From politics to religion was at that time an easy transition, and this powerful poem, which is in the form of an epistle to his friend Henry Dickenson, is at once a vindication of Revealed as distinguished from Natural Religion, and an appeal to Christians not to confound what is essential and vital in religious truth with what is accidental and of secondary importance. It is a defence of the Church of England against the Papists and the Sectaries, by one who had satisfied himself of the social and political importance of a State religion, but who had satisfied himself of little else.

It is strange and melancholy to find the author of poems so brilliant, so powerful, and so popular, condemned by the meanness of his royal and aristocratic patrons to toil like a hack in a Grub Street garret. Yet so it was.

His salary as Poet Laureate was in arrears. His income
from the theatres was considerably diminished. His
health was impaired, and a visit into the country was,
as his physician informed him, not only desirable but
necessary. His means, however, were at such a low ebb
that without relief it was impossible for him to leave
London. He was even in danger of being arrested for
debt. "Be pleased to look on me," he wrote about
this time to Rochester, "with an eye of compassion.
Some small employment would make my condition
easy"; and he adds bitterly, "'Tis enough for one age
to have neglected Mr. Cowley and starved Mr. Butler."
His appeal was successful; and he was appointed (December 17th, 1683) to an office once held by Chaucer, the
Collectorship of Customs in the port of London. Mean-
while his pen was not idle. In 1683 he concluded a
Preface and a Life of Plutarch to the translation of the
Lives by several hands. In 1684 he translated, by order
of the King, Maimbourg's *History of the League;* at the
beginning of the same year he brought out a volume of
Miscellanies, and in the following year a second volume
containing versions from Virgil, Horace, Lucretius, and
Theocritus. In February, 1685, died Charles II., and
Dryden, as Poet Laureate, mourned him in a frigid
"Pindaric" ode, the *Threnodia Augustalis*. Eleven
months after the new king had ascended the throne
Evelyn entered in his Diary, "Dryden, the famous
play-writer, and his two sons, and Mrs. Nelly (miss
to the late king) were said to go to mass; such pro-
selytes were no great loss to the Church." With regard
to Mrs. Nelly, Evelyn had been misinformed; the
Church was not to lose her, she was to adorn it till her

death. With regard to Dryden his information was correct. The Poet Laureate had indeed publicly embraced the creed which his royal master was labouring to uphold, and his salary was at once raised to its full amount. This is not the place to discuss the question of Dryden's probable sincerity or insincerity in his conversion to a creed which had hitherto been a favourite butt of his sarcastic wit. It is, however, doing him no more than justice to say that there is not the smallest reason for supposing that he either gained or anticipated that he would gain anything by his apostasy; that his salary would in all probability have been raised had he remained a Protestant; that he found in the Ancient Church what he desiderated in the *Religio Laici;* that during the rest of his life, and on his death-bed, where few men are hypocrites, he professed that he felt a satisfaction such as he had not before known, and that he never recanted though recantation would have been to his advantage.

Neither the king nor the leaders of the Roman Catholic party were likely to allow so accomplished a controversialist as their new ally to remain inactive, and Dryden was soon in the arena. An unimportant but singularly intemperate controversy with Stillingfleet, the Dean of St. Paul's, was the prelude to a controversy to which we owe what is on the whole the most magnificent of his poems, *The Hind and Panther.* No act had more enraged and perplexed the friends of the Constitution in Church and State than the king's recent assumption of the dispensing power, to which he was now about to give practical expression in the Declaration of Indulgence. Dryden's object in this allegory was threefold. It was to vindicate the king's right to the assumption of that power, in other words, to vindicate the Declaration: it was to prove that the religion of Christians, if pure and sound, is and can only be the religion of the Church of Rome, or at least a religion which is in essentials the same: it was to denounce and expose the errors of Protestant-ism, and especially those of the Sectaries. The frame-work of this poem has been not unnaturally ridiculed, and Dryden at the beginning of the Third Part en-deavoured to anticipate the objections of censorious critics by adducing the examples of Æsop and Spenser, and he might have added that of Chaucer. He is said to have been greatly annoyed at the ludicrous travesty of his work by Prior and Montague—*The Hind and the Panther Transversed*. The last service he was destined to perform for James II. was the com-position of the poem on the birth of the unfortunate Prince of Wales (June 10th, 1688), the *Britannia Rediviva*, the most eloquent of his official productions. A few months afterwards James II. was in exile, and William and Mary on the throne.

1688-1700.

By the Revolution Dryden lost everything but what remained of his private fortune and what he had con-trived to save. He was deprived of the Laureateship, and he had the mortification of seeing his old enemy Shadwell succeeding him. He was deprived of the His-toriographership and of his place in the Customs. From all hope of preferment he was absolutely excluded. He was moreover far in the decline of life, and his health was breaking. For the support of an expensive family and an expensive town-house he had now nothing but his pen to depend on. Incessant drudgery, even till the end came, was to be his lot. But if Fortune had been cruel Nature was kind. The decay of his physical powers had no appreciable effect on his intellect and his genius, both of which were as bright and vigorous as in his most palmy days. Indeed his fertility of production was wonderful. He first betook himself to dramatic composition, and in 1690 appeared his masterpiece in tragedy *Don Sebastian*. This was succeeded in the same year by a successful comedy, *Amphitryon*. Then came (1691) a dramatic opera, *King Arthur*, and in the summer of the same year he completed *Cleomenes*. With *Love Triumphant* (1694), a comedy which was a failure, he took leave of the stage for ever. Meanwhile he had published (Feb. 1691-2) his fine funeral poem on the death of the Countess of Abingdon, entitled *Eleonora*. In 1693 appeared the translation of the *Satires* of Juvenal and Persius; of Juvenal's satires he himself translated the first, third, sixth, tenth, and sixteenth, but in the version of Persius he had no assistance. And to this work he prefixed one of the best of his critical treatises, the *Essay on Satire*. Between 1693 and the end of 1694 he published two volumes of *Miscellanies*, and between 1693 and 1697 he translated the whole of *Virgil*. This work has attained with Pope's *Homer* a reputation such as no other translation in our language has attained. They are the only versions of classics which have themselves become classical. Nor is this fame undeserved. Marred by coarseness, marred

by miserable inequalities, marred by reckless careless-
ness, Dryden's *Virgil* is still a memorable achievement,
a work such as no man of mere ability could possibly
have produced.   It is a work instinct with genius, not
with the placid and majestic genius of · the artist
whom Tennyson loved and resembles, but with the
masculine and impetuous energy of the prince of
English rhetorical poets.   As usual, Dryden enriched
the work with one of his charming critical dissertations,
the *Essay on Epic Poetry*.   The old poet was pleased
with the reception of his work.   " My *Virgil*," he
wrote to his sons at Rome, "succeeds in the world
beyond its desert or my reputation."   It was just
after the appearance of his *Virgil* that he composed his famous lyric, *Alexander's Feast*, a lyric
which, in spite of its fame, is far inferior to his
first *Ode on St. Cecilia's Day* and to his *Ode to the
Memory of Mrs. Anne Killigrew*.   His last important
production was what is known as the *Fables*, written
in accordance with an agreement with his publisher,
Tonson, to supply him with 10,000 verses for the sum
of 250 guineas.   In this work he versifies the stories
of Sigismonda and Guiscardo, Theodore and Honoria,
Cymon and Iphigenia from Boccaccio's *Decameron*, and
paraphrases, in his own style, Chaucer's *Knights Tale*,
Nun Priest's Tale, and *Wife of Bath's Tale*, *Character
of the Good Parson*, and *The Flower and the Leaf*, pre-
facing the work with a graceful dedicatory epistle to
the Duchess of Ormond, and adding one of the most
precious of · his critical essays.

It is pleasing and yet melancholy to turn to Dryden's
private life during these years.   His contract with

Tonson sufficiently proves how wretchedly he was paid for his arduous and incessant drudgery, and his letters and dedications are full of complaints about his poverty, his ill-health, and the malice of his enemies. But he had many solaces. Personally he appears to have been a very amiable and very sociable man, the fondest of fathers, the kindest of friends. Many anecdotes are extant of his goodness to young authors and aspirants to literary fame, who repaid him with an affection which has more than once found most touching expression. He was a welcome guest wherever he chose to visit, and many of the most delightful houses in England were open to him. As he drew near his end he is said to have expressed great regret at the immoral tendency of some of his writings, and his only retort to Collier's savage attack on him in the *Short View of the Profaneness and Immorality of the English Stage* was an acknowledgment of its justice: "If he be my enemy let him triumph. If he be my friend, and I have given him no personal occasion to be otherwise, he will be glad of my repentance."

On the 30th of April, 1700, it was announced in a London newspaper that "John Dryden, the famous poet, lies a-dying." He had been told by his physicians that a not very painful operation would save his life. He chose rather to resign it. "He received," said one who saw him die, "the notice of his approaching dissolution with sweet submission and entire resignation to the Divine will, and he took so tender and obliging a farewell of his friends as none but himself could have expressed." He breathed his last on the 1st of May, 1700. His body lay in state for several days in the College

of Physicians, and on May the 13th was honoured with a
public funeral more imposing and magnificent than any
which had been conceded to an English poet before.
He was laid in the Great Abbey by the dust of Chaucer
and Spenser, not far from the graves of his old friend
Davenant and his old schoolmaster Busby.

INTRODUCTION TO
ABSALOM AND ACHITOPHEL.

FROM the fall of Clarendon in August, 1667, to the death of Shaftesbury in January, 1683, England was in a high state of ferment and agitation. The mad joy of 1660 had undergone its natural reaction, and this reaction was intensified by a long series of national calamities and political blunders. There were feuds in the Cabinet and among the people; the religion of the country was in imminent peril; the Royal house had become a centre of perfidy and disaffection. Clarendon had been made the scape-goat of the disasters which marked the commencement of the reign, of the miserable squabbles attendant on the Act of Indemnity, of the first Dutch War, of the Sale of Dunkirk; but Clarendon was now in exile, and with him was removed one of the very few honourable ministers in the service of the Stuarts. The Triple Alliance (April, 1668) was followed by the scandalous Treaty of. Dover (May, 1670), by which an English king bound himself to re-establish the Roman Catholic religion in England, and to join his arms with those of the French king in support of the House of Bourbon, that he might turn the arms of France against his own subjects, should they attempt to oppose his designs. Between the end of 1667 and the beginning of 1674 the government was in the hands of the Cabal, the most unprincipled and profligate ministry in the annals of our constitutional history. Then followed the administration of Danby. Danby, with all his faults, had the honesty to exchange the shuffling and ignominious tactics of the Cabal for cordial and consistent hatred of the French abroad and of Papists and Nonconformists at home. The Peace of Nimeguen (August, 1678) threw England back on herself. Danby fell, partly because no minister at such a time could hold his own for long, mainly owing to the machinations of Louis XIV., who was to the England of Charles II. what his predecessor Louis XI. had been to the Switzerland of Charles the Bold, and to the England of Edward IV. From a jarring chaos of Cavaliers, Puritans, Roman Catholics, Presbyterians, country parties, of colliding interests, of maddened Commons, of a corrupted and corrupting ministry, of a disaffected Church, of plots and counter-plots, of a Royal house ostensibly in opposition, but secretly in union, two great parties had been gradually defining themselves.

In May, 1662, the king had married Catharine of Braganza, but he had no issue by her, and as she had now (1679) been his wife for seventeen years they were not likely to have issue, and the question of the succession began to assume prominence. In the event of the king leaving no legitimate children the crown would revert to the Duke of York. But the Duke of York was a Papist, and of all the many prejudices of the English people generally, the prejudice against Papacy was strongest. All now began to centre on this question, and two great parties were formed. The one party insisted on the exclusion of the Duke of York from the right of succession, on the ground of his religion. These were the Petitioners, afterwards nicknamed Whigs, and the Exclusionists; their leader was the Earl of Shaftesbury. The other party, strongest among Churchmen and the aristocracy, were anxious, partly in accordance with the theory of the divine right of kings and the duty of passive obedience, and partly with an eye to their own interests, to please the king by supporting the claim of his brother. These were the Abhorrers, afterwards nicknamed Tories. The object of the Exclusionists was to inflame the populace against the Papists. For this purpose the infamous fictions of Oates and his accomplices were accepted and promulgated (September, 1678), and the complications which succeeded the fall of Danby took their rise. These were succeeded by a second attempt to exasperate the public mind against the Anti-Exclusionists, which found expression in the Meal-Tub Plot (June, 1680). But to turn to the principal actors in this great public drama.

Anthony Ashley Cooper was the eldest son of Sir John Cooper, and was born July 22, 1621, at Winburne, St. Giles. At the age of fifteen he became a Fellow Commoner of Exeter College, Oxford. On quitting Oxford he removed to Lincoln's Inn, where he acquired that knowledge of constitutional law and history for which, throughout his life, he was celebrated. While still in the nineteenth year he represented in Parliament the town of Tewkesbury. At the beginning of the Civil War he served the king in many important posts, though he does not seem to have gained the entire confidence of his party. Piqued in all probability by a slight on the part of Prince Maurice, or, according to his own account, perceiving that the king's aim was "destructive to religion and the state," he went over, early in 1644, to the Parliamentary side, becoming, as Lord Clarendon says, "an implacable enemy to the Royal family." Shortly afterwards we find him intriguing with the Royalists though holding responsible posts under the Parliament. He was a member of Cromwell's Council of State, but was frequently in opposition to him, and, on the Protector's death, was one of the first to assail him with scurrilous abuse. From the death of Cromwell to the Restoration he filled important offices under the Parliament, and carried on a surreptitious - correspondence with the Royalists. Ever foremost where interest led we find him one of the twelve members of the House of Commons who were in the spring of 1660 sent over to Holland to invite the king to England. At the Restoration he was rewarded for his loyalty by being created Baron Ashley. It is difficult to follow him through the complicated political history of the next few years, or to pronounce with any certainty whether he was or was not guilty of the many delinquencies which have been imputed to him. His anxious apologist, Mr. Christie, contends that he was not privy to the king's scandalous secret treaty with France, and asserts that so far from promoting the infamous Closure of the Exchequer he strongly opposed it. He was, however, a leading mem-

ber of the ministry (the Cabal) which was responsible
for this measure.   In 1672 he was created Baron
Cooper of Pawlet, in Somerset, and Earl of Shaftesbury, and was at the same time Chancellor and Under-
Treasurer of the Exchequer.   In November of the
following year he was promoted to the Woolsack.   As
Lord Chancellor he acquitted himself with signal ability,
and gained the reputation of being diligent, judicious,
honest, and impartial.   By skilfully adapting himself to
the king's humours he was able, for a time, not only to
maintain his perilously uncertain position, but to gain
opportunities for furthering his ambitious and complicated schemes which were soon afterwards unfolded.
While Lord Chancellor he had the misfortune—if he
did not seek the opportunity—to quarrel with the Duke
of York.   James had doubtless perceived that Shaftesbury's schemes were not likely to coincide with his
own, and that the Chancellor was not the man to
hazard fortune by furthering the cause of popery.   By
the Duke's manœuvres, therefore, Shaftesbury was forced
to resign the Great Seal, though he still sat in Parliament.   Shaftesbury's leading principle now became
hatred for the Duke of York and popery; and he
determined to secure, if possible, the succession for
Monmouth, the king's son by Lucy Walters.   With
this object he attempted to gain the confidence of the
people and of the king.   The people, as he well knew,
detested Roman Catholics, and had no affection for
the Duke of York.   Monmouth, though known to be
the king's illegitimate child, was a popular favourite,
and, indifferent to all religions, became, under the
auspices of Shaftesbury and with the prospect of a crown,

the representative of Protestantism. A wild story was circulated that Charles had made Lucy Walters his wife. Monmouth himself was, in many respects, well fitted to play the part Shaftesbury wished him to support. His manners were singularly engaging, his disposition affable, his character, with all its weakness, manly. He had served two campaigns in Louis XIV.'s army against the Dutch, and had greatly distinguished himself. Of his person we have a very graphic description in Hamilton's *Memoirs*—"His figure and the exterior graces of his form were such that nature perhaps never framed anything more complete. His face was eminently handsome, and yet it was a manly face, neither inanimate nor effeminate." At the end of November, 1679, Monmouth arrived in England, and entering London was received with enthusiastic applause. Simultaneously with his appearance his partizans, prompted no doubt by Shaftesbury, circulated "An appeal from the country to the city for the preservation of his majesty's person, liberty, property, and religion." It pointed out that what was needed was a man to lead true-hearted Britons against French invaders and popish rebels, and that that man was Monmouth, qualified alike by birth, conduct, and courage. His fortune, it continued, was united with theirs, and citizens would do well to remember that "the worst title makes the best king." Every month added to the popular excitement, and Shaftesbury at the head of the stormy democracy of the city was now sanguine of success. All centred on the Exclusion Bill, which, on the 11th of November, 1680, triumphantly passed the Commons, but was defeated in the Lords. The country was now on the verge of civil war. Parliament was dissolved in January, 1681, and such was the frenzy in London that the next Parliament was summoned to meet at Oxford. It met, amid storm and tumult, in the following March, but was suddenly dissolved, without transacting business. The fear of civil war, now imminent, brought on a reaction, and the king soon found himself strong enough to strike a decisive blow against the arch-enemy of the public peace. In July, Shaftesbury was arrested on a charge of "subornation of high treason for conspiring for the death of the king and the subversion of the Government," and thrown into the Tower to await his trial at the Old Bailey in the following November. At this momentous crisis, just a week before the trial on which so much depended, appeared *Absalom and Achitophel.* Well might Sir Walter Scott observe that "the time of its appearance was chosen with as much art as the poem displays genius."

Absalom and Achitophel forms an era in the history of English classical satire. Satire had passed successively through the hands of Gascoign* (1576), Donne (1593-1602), Lodge (1595), Hall (1597-8), Marston (1598), Wither (1611), Cleveland (1647), Marvel (*circ.* 1667); Oldham (whose *Satires upon the Jesuits* preceded Dryden's poem two years); but it had never attained an excellence comparable to what it attained here. It raised English satire indeed to the level of that superb satirical literature which Quintilian claimed as the peculiar and exclusive product of Roman genius. Not only did it furnish Pope and the school of

---

* The dates given are the dates of the appearance of the principal satires of the particular writers.

Pope, as well as Akenside, Smollet, Churchill, Gifford, Byron, and others, with models, but it exhibited for the first time the power, plasticity, and compass of the heroic couplet in departments of poetry where it was to achieve its greatest triumphs. The plan of the poem is not perhaps original. The idea of casting satire in the epic mould, which is an important feature of the work, was suggested no doubt by the fourth satire of Juvenal. Horace and Lucan undoubtedly supplied models for the elaborate portraits, and Lucan's description of the political condition of Rome at the time of the great civil conflict is, unmistakably, Dryden's archetype for his picture of the state of parties in London. Nor was the ingenious device of disguising living persons and current incidents and analogies under the veil of Scriptural names new to his readers. A Roman Catholic poet, for example, had, in 1679, paraphrased the Scriptural story of Naboth's vineyard, applying it to the condemnation of Lord Strafford for his supposed complicity in the Popish Plot, while a small prose tract, published at Dublin in 1680, entitled *Absalom's Conspiracy; or, The Tragedy of Treason*, anticipates in adumbration the very scheme of his work. But the analogy between Jewish history in the reign of David (cf. II. of Samuel, from verse 25 of the 14th chapter to the end of chapter 18), and the condition of England in 1681—the analogy between David, Absalom. and Achitophel on the one hand, and between Charles II., Monmouth, and Shaftes- bury on the other—were sufficiently obvious to strike a less intelligent reader than Dryden. This poem is the triumph of genius as distinguished from mere talent, for the verdict of those whom it delighted, as actors and spectators in the world which it mirrors, has been corroborated by the judgment of those to whom what is local and ephemeral in it has long ceased to be of interest. A party pamphlet,—in the hands of Regnier or Churchill a party pamphlet it would have remained,— that and nothing more Let the student ask himself, or ask his teachers, why Dryden's party pamphlet is immortal.

ABSALOM AND ACHITOPHEL.

A POEM.

"Si propius stes
Te capiat magis."
HORACE, *Ars Poet.* 361.

TO THE READER.

'TIS not my intention to make an apology for my poem : some will think it needs no excuse, and others will receive none. The design, I am sure, is honest ; but he who draws his pen for one party must expect to make enemies of the other. For wit and fool are consequents of Whig and Tory ; and every man is a knave or an ass to the contrary side. There's a treasury of merits in the Fanatic church as well as in the Papist, and a pennyworth to be had of saintship, honesty, and poetry, for the lewd, the factious, and the blockheads ; but the longest chapter in Deuteronomy has 10 not curses enough for an Anti-Bromingham. My comfort is, their manifest prejudice to my cause will render their judgment of less authority against me. Yet if a poem have a genius, it will force its own reception in the world ; for there is a sweetness in good verse, which tickles even while it hurts ; and no man can be heartily angry with him who pleases him against his will. The commendation of adversaries is the greatest triumph of a writer, because it never comes unless extorted. But I can be satisfied on more easy

Œ   A

terms : if I happen to please the more moderate sort, I shall
be sure of an honest party and, in all probability, of the
best judges ; for the least concerned are commonly the least
corrupt. And I confess I have laid in for those, by rebating
the satire, where justice would allow it, from carrying too
sharp an edge. They who can criticize so weakly as to
imagine I have done my worst, may be convinced at their
own cost that I can write severely with more ease than I can
gently. I have but laughed at some men's follies, when I
10 could have declaimed against their vices ; and other men's
virtues I have commended as freely as I have taxed their
crimes. And now, if you are a malicious reader, I expect
you should return upon me that I affect to be thought more
impartial than I am ; but if men are not to be judged by
their professions, God forgive you commonwealth's-men for
professing so plausibly for the government. You cannot be
so unconscionable as to charge me for not subscribing of my
name ; for that would reflect too grossly upon your own
party, who never dare, though they have the advantage of a
20 jury to secure them. If you like not my poem, the fault
may possibly be in my writing, though 'tis hard for an
author to judge against himself ; but more probably 'tis in
your morals, which cannot bear the truth of it. The violent
on both sides will condemn the character of Absalom, as
either too favourably or too hardly drawn ; but they are not
the violent whom I desire to please. The fault on the right
hand is to extenuate, palliate, and indulge ; and, to confess
freely, I have endeavoured to commit it. Besides the respect
which I owe his birth, I have a greater for his heroic virtues ;
30 and David himself could not be more tender of the young
man's life, than I would be of his reputation. But since the
most excellent natures are always the most easy and, as
being such, are the soonest perverted by ill counsels, especially when baited with fame and glory, it is no more a
wonder that he withstood not the temptations of Achitophel
than it was for Adam not to have resisted the two devils,

the serpent and the woman. The conclusion of the story I
purposely forebore to prosecute, because I could not obtain
from myself to show Absalom unfortunate. The frame of
it was cut out but for a picture to the waist ; and if the
draught be so far true, it is as much as I designed.

Were I the inventor, who am only the historian, I should
certainly conclude the piece with the reconcilement of
Absalom to David. And who knows but this may come
to pass ? Things were not brought to an extremity where
I left the story : there seems yet to be room left for a 10
composure ; hereafter there may only be for pity. I have
not so much as an uncharitable wish against Achitophel,
but am content to be accused of a good-natured error, and
to hope with Origen, that the Devil himself may at last be
saved. For which reason, in this poem, he is neither
brought to set his house in order, nor to dispose of his
person afterwards as he in wisdom shall think fit. God is
infinitely merciful ; and his vicegerent is only not so,
because he is not infinite.

The true end of satire is the amendment of vices by 20
correction. And he who writes honestly is no more an
enemy to the offender than the physician to the patient,
when he prescribes harsh remedies to an inveterate disease ;
for those are only in order to prevent the chirurgeon's work
of an *Ense rescindendum*, which I wish not to my very
enemies. To conclude all ; if the body politic have any
analogy to the natural, in my weak judgment, an act of
oblivion were as necessary in a hot distempered state as
an opiate would be in a raging fever.   29

ABSALOM AND ACHITOPHEL.

In pious times, ere priestcraft did begin,
Before polygamy was made a sin,
When man on many multiplied his kind,
Ere one to one was cursedly confined, . .
Then Israel's monarch after Heaven's own heart
His vigorous warmth did variously impart
To wives and slaves, and, wide as his command,
Scattered his Maker's image through the land.   10
Michal, of royal blood, the crown did wear,
A soil ungrateful to the tiller's care :
Not so the rest ; for several mothers bore
To god-like David several sons before.
But since like slaves his bed they did ascend,
No true succession could their seed attend.
Of all this numerous progeny was none
So beautiful, so brave, as Absalon   20
For that his conscious destiny made way
By manly beauty to imperial sway.
Early in foreign fields he won renown
With kings and states allied to Israel's crown :
In peace the thoughts of war he could remove
And seemed as he were only born for love.

4

Whate'er he did was done with so much ease,
In him alone 'twas natural to please;
His motions all accompanied with grace,
And Paradise was opened in his face.   30
With secret joy indulgent David viewed
His youthful image in his son renewed;
To all his wishes nothing he denied
And made the charming Annabel his bride.
What faults he had (for who from faults is free?)
His father could not or he would not see.
Some warm excesses, which the law forbore,
Were construed youth that purged by boiling o'er;
And Amnon's murder by a specious name
Was called a just revenge for injured fame.   40
Thus praised and loved, the noble youth remained,
While David undisturbed in Sion reigned.
But life can never be sincerely blest;
Heaven punishes the bad, and proves the best.
The Jews, a headstrong, moody, murmuring race
As ever tried the extent and stretch of grace;
God's pampered people, whom, debauched with ease
No king could govern nor no God could please;
Gods they had tried of every shape and size
That godsmiths could produce or priests devise;   50
These Adam-wits, too fortunately free,
Began to dream they wanted liberty;
And when no rule, no precedent was found
Of men by laws less circumscribed and bound,
They led their wild desires to woods and caves
And thought that all but savages were slaves.
They who, when Saul was dead, without a blow
Made foolish Ishbosheth the crown forego;
Who banished David did from Hebron bring,
And with a general shout proclaimed him King;   60
Those very Jews who at their very best
Their humour more than loyalty exprest,

Now wondered why so long they had obeyed
An idol monarch which their hands had made ;
Thought they might ruin him they could create
Or melt him to that golden calf, a State.
But these were random bolts ; no formed design
Nor interest made the factious crowd to join :
The sober part of Israel, free from stain,
Well knew the value of a peaceful reign ;   70
And looking backward with a wise affright
Saw seams of wounds dishonest to the sight,
In contemplation of whose ugly scars
They cursed the memory of civil wars.
The moderate sort of men, thus qualified,
Inclined the balance to the better side ;
And David's mildness managed it so well,
The bad found no occasion to rebel.
But when to sin our biassed nature leans,
The careful Devil is still at hand with means   80
And providently pimps for ill desires :
The good old cause, revived, a plot requires,
Plots true or false are necessary things,
To raise up commonwealths and u kings.
  The inhabitants of old Jerusalem
Were Jebusites ; the town so called from them,
And theirs the native right.
But when the chosen people grew more strong,
The rightful cause at length became the wrong ;
And every loss the men of Jebus bore,   90
They still were thought God's enemies the more.
Thus worn and weakened, well or ill content,
Submit they must to David's government :
Impoverished and deprived of all command,
Their taxes doubled as they lost their land ;
And, what was harder yet to flesh and blood,
Their gods disgraced, and burnt like common wood.

This set the heathen priesthood in a flame,
For priests of all religions are the same.
Of whatsoe'er descent their godhead be,   100
Stock, stone, or other homely pedigree,
In his defence his servants are as bold,
As if he had been born of beaten gold.
The Jewish Rabbins, though their enemies,
In this conclude them honest men and wise :
For 'twas their duty, all the learned think,
To espouse his cause by whom they eat and drink.
From hence began that Plot, the nation's curse,
Bad in itself, but represented worse,
Raised in extremes, and in extremes decried,   110
With oaths affirmed, with dying vows denied
Not weighed or winnowed by the multitude,
But swallowed in the mass, unchewed and crude.
Some truth there was, but dashed and brewed with lies
To please the fools and puzzle all the wise :
Succeeding times did equal folly call
Believing nothing or believing all.
The Egyptian rites the Jebusites embraced,
Where gods were recommended by their taste ;
Such savoury deities must needs be good   120
As served at once for worship and for food,
By force they could not introduce these gods,
For ten to one in former days was odds :
So fraud was used, the sacrificer's trade ;
Fools are more hard to conquer than persuade.
Their busy teachers mingled with the Jews
And raked for converts even the court and stews
Which Hebrew priests the more unkindly took,
Because the fleece accompanies the flock.
Some thought they God's anointed meant to slay   130
By guns, invented since full many a day :
Our author swears it not ; but who can know
How far the Devil and Jebusites may go ?

This plot, which failed for want of common sense,
Had yet a deep and dangerous consequence ;
For as, when raging fevers boil the blood,
The standing lake soon floats into a flood,
And every hostile humour which before
Slept quiet in its channels bubbles o'er ;
So several factions from this first ferment   140
Work up to foam and threat the government.
Some by their friends, more by themselves thought wise,
Opposed the power to which they could not rise.
Some had in courts been great and, thrown from thence,
Like fiends were hardened in impenitence.
Some by their Monarch's fatal mercy grown
From pardoned rebels kinsmen to the throne
Were raised in power and public office high ;
Strong bands, if bands ungrateful men could tie.
Of these the false Achitophel was first,   150
A name to all succeeding ages curst :
For close designs and crooked counsels fit,
Sagacious, bold, and turbulent of wit,
Restless, unfixed in principles and place,
In power unpleased, impatient of disgrace ;
A fiery soul, which working out its way,
Fretted the pigmy body to decay
And o'er-informed the tenement of clay.
A daring pilot in extremity,
Pleased with the danger, when the waves went high,   160
He sought the storms ; but, for a calm unfit,
Would steer too nigh the sands to boast his wit.
Great wits are sure to madness near allied
And thin partitions do their bounds divide ;
Else, why should he, with wealth and honour blest,
Refuse his age the needful hours of rest ?
Punish a body which he could not please,
Bankrupt of life, yet prodigal of ease ?
And all to leave what with his toil he won

To that unfeathered two-legged thing, a son, 170
Got, while his soul did huddled notions try,
And born a shapeless lump, like anarchy.
In friendship false, implacable in hate,
Resolved to ruin or to rule the state ;
To compass this the triple bond he broke,
The pillars of the public safety shook,
And fitted Israel for a foreign yoke ;
Then, seized with fear, yet still affecting fame,
Usurped a patriot's all-atoning name.
So easy still it proves in factious times 180
With public zeal to cancel private crimes.
How safe is treason and how sacred ill,
Where none can sin against the people's will,
Where crowds can wink and no offence be known,
Since in another's guilt they find their own !
Yet fame deserved no enemy can grudge ;
The statesman we abhor, but praise the judge —
In Israel's courts ne'er sat an Abbethdin
With more discerning eyes or hands more clean,
Unbribed, unsought, the wretched to redress,
Swift of despatch and easy of access.
Oh ! had he been content to serve the crown
With virtues only proper to the gown,
Or had the rankness of the soil been freed
From cockle that oppressed the noble seed,
David for him his tuneful harp had strung
And Heaven had wanted one immortal song.
But wild ambition loves to slide, not stand,
And Fortune's ice prefers to Virtue's land.
Achitophel, grown weary to possess 200
A lawful fame and lazy happiness,
Disdained the golden fruit to gather free
And lent the crowd his arm to shake the tree.
Now, manifest of crimes contrived long since,
He stood at bold defiance with his Prince,

Held up the buckler of the people's cause
Against the crown, and skulked behind the laws.
The wished occasion of the Plot he takes ;
Some circumstances finds, but more he makes ;
By buzzing emissaries fills the ears   210
Of listening crowds with jealousies and fears
Of arbitrary counsels brought to light,
And proves the King himself a Jebusite.
Weak arguments ! which yet he knew full well
Were strong with people easy to rebel.
For governed by the moon, the giddy Jews
Tread the same track when she the prime renews
And once in twenty years their scribes record,
By natural instinct they change their lord.
Achitophel still wants a chief, and none   220
Was found so fit as warlike Absalon.
Not that he wished his greatness to create,
For politicians neither love nor hate :
But, for he knew his title not allowed
Would keep him still depending on the crowd,
That kingly power, thus ebbing out, might be
Drawn to the dregs of a democracy.
Him he attempts with studied arts to please
And sheds his venom in such words as these

" Auspicious prince, at whose nativity   230
" Some royal planet ruled the southern sky,
" Thy longing country's darling and desire,
" Their cloudy pillar and their guardian fire,
" Their second Moses, whose extended wand
" Divides the seas and shows the promised land,
" Whose dawning day in every distant age
" Has exercised the sacred prophet's rage,
" The people's prayer, the glad diviner's theme,
" The young men's vision, and the old men's dream,
" Thee Saviour, thee the nation's vows confess,   240

*make up this speech — to intermost
Shaftsbury's rebellion*

*Artisue
sly un*

*D. states not clearly, issues at stake
this time.*

"And never satisfied with seeing bless :
"Swift unbespoken pomps thy steps proclaim,
"And stammering babes are taught to lisp thy name.
"How long wilt thou the general joy detain,
"Starve and defraud the people of thy reign ?
"Content ingloriously to pass thy days,
"Like one of virtue's fools that feeds on praise ;
"Till thy fresh glories, which now shine so bright,
"Grow stale and tarnish with our daily sight.
"Believe me, royal youth, thy fruit must be   250
"Or gathered ripe, or rot upon the tree.
"Heaven has to all allotted, soon or late,
"Some lucky revolution of their fate :
"Whose motions if we watch and guide with skill,
"(For human good depends on human will,)
"Our fortune rolls as from a smooth descent
"And from the first impression takes the bent ;
"But, if unseized, she glides away like wind
"And leaves repenting folly far behind.
"Now, now she meets you with a glorious prize   260
"And spreads her locks before her as she flies.
"Had thus old David, from whose loins you spring,
"Not dared, when Fortune called him to be King,
"At Gath an exile he might still remain,
"And Heaven's anointing oil had been in vain.
"Let his successful youth your hopes engage,
"But shun the example of declining age.
"Behold him setting in his western skies,
"The shadows lengthening as the vapours rise ;
"He is not now, as when, on Jordan's sand,   270
"The joyful people thronged to see him land,
"Covering the beach and blackening all the strand,
"But like the Prince of Angels, from his height
"Comes tumbling downward with diminished light :
"Betrayed by one poor Plot to public scorn,
"(Our only blessing since his curst return,)

"Those heaps of people, which one sheaf did bind,
"Blown off and scattered by a puff of wind.
"What strength can he to your designs oppose,
"Naked of friends, and round beset with foes?   280
"If Pharaoh's doubtful succour he should use,
"A foreign aid would more incense the Jews;
"Proud Egypt would dissembled friendship bring
"Foment the war, but not support the King
"Nor would the royal party e'er unite
"With Pharaoh's arms to assist the Jebusite;
"Or, if they should, their interest soon would break
"And with such odious aid make David weak.
"All sorts of men, by my successful arts
"Abhorring kings, estrange their altered hearts   290
"From David's rule: and 'tis the general cry,
"Religion, commonwealth, and liberty.
"If you, as champion of the public good,
"Add to their arms a chief of royal blood,
"What may not Israel hope, and what applause
"Might such a general gain by such a cause?
"Not barren praise alone, that gaudy flower,
"Fair only to the sight, but solid power;
"And nobler is a limited command,
"Given by the love of all your native land,   300
"Than a successive title, long and dark,
"Drawn from the mouldy rolls of Noah's ark."

What cannot praise effect in mighty minds,
When flattery soothes and when ambition blinds?
Desire of power, on earth a vicious weed,
Yet sprung from high is of celestial seed;
In God 'tis glory, and when men aspire,
'Tis but a spark too much of heavenly fire.
The ambitious youth, too covetous of fame,
Too full of angel's metal in his frame,   310
Unwarily was led from virtue's ways,

Made drunk with honour and debauched with praise.
Half loth and half consenting to the ill,
For loyal blood within him struggled still,
He thus replied : " And what pretence have I
" To take up arms for public liberty ?
" My father governs with unquestioned right,
" The faith's defender and mankind's delight,
" Good, gracious, just, observant of the laws ;
" And Heaven by wonders has espoused his cause.   320
" Whom has he wronged in all his peaceful reign ?
" Who sues for justice to his throne in vain ?
" What millions has he pardoned of his foes
" Whom just revenge did to his wrath expose.
" Mild, easy, humble, studious of our good,
" Inclined to mercy and averse from blood.
" If mildness ill with stubborn Israel suit,
" His crime is God's beloved attribute.
" What could he gain his people to betray
" Or change his right for arbitrary sway ?   330
" Let haughty Pharaoh curse with such a reign
" His fruitful Nile, and yoke a servile train.
" If David's rule Jerusalem displease,
" The dog-star heats their brains to this disease.
" Why then should I, encouraging the bad,
" Turn rebel and run popularly mad ?
" Were he a tyrant, who by lawless might
" Oppressed the Jews·and raised the Jebusite,
" Well might I mourn ; but nature's holy bands
" Would curb my spirits and restrain my hands ;   340
" The people might assert their liberty,
" But what was right in them were crime in me.
" His favour leaves me nothing to require
" Prevents my wishes and outruns desire ;
" What more can I expect while David lives ?
" All but his kingly diadem he gives :
" And that "—But there he paused, then sighing said,

" Is justly destined for a worthier head ;
" For when my father from his toils shall rest
" And late augment the number of the blest,   350
" His lawful issue shall the throne ascend,
" Or the collateral line, where that shall end.
" His brother, though oppressed with vulgar spite,
" Yet dauntless and secure of native right,
" Of every royal virtue stands possest,
" Still dear to all the bravest and the best.
" His courage foes, his friends his truth proclaim,
" His loyalty the King, the world his fame.
" His mercy even the offending crowd will find,
" For sure he comes of a forgiving kind.   360
" Why should I then rapine at Heaven's decree
" Which gives me no pretence to royalty ?
" Yet oh that Fate, propitiously inclined,
" Had raised my birth or had debased my mind,
" To my large soul not all her treasure lent,
" And then betrayed it to a mean descent !
" I find, I find my mounting spirits bold,
" And David's part disdains my mother's mould.
" Why am I scanted by a niggard birth ?
" My soul disclaims the kindred of her earth   370
" And, made for empire, whispers me within.
" Desire of greatness is a god-like sin."

Him staggering so when Hell's dire agent found,
While fainting virtue scarce maintained her ground,
He pours fresh forces in, and thus replies :
    " The eternal God, supremely good and wise,
" Imparts not these prodigious gifts in vain.
" What wonders are reserved to bless your reign !
" Against your will your arguments have shown,
" Such virtue's only given to guide a throne.   380
" Not that your father's mildness I contemn,
" But manly force becomes the diadem.

" 'Tis true he grants the people all they crave,
" And more perhaps than subjects ought to have :
" For lavish grants suppose a monarch tame
" And more his goodness than his wit proclaim.
" But when should people strive their bonds to break,
" If not when kings are negligent or weak ?
" Let him give on till he can give no more,
" The thrifty Sanhedrin shall keep him poor ;   390
" And every shekel which he can receive
" Shall cost a limb of his prerogative.
" To ply him with new plots shall be my care,
" Or plunge him deep in some expensive war ;
" Which when his treasure can no more supply,
" He must with the remains of kingship buy.
" His faithful friends our jealousies and fears
" Call Jebusites and Pharaoh's pensioners,
" Whom when our fury from his aid has torn,
" He shall be naked left to public scorn.   400
" The next successor, whom I fear and hate,
" My arts have made obnoxious to the State,
" Turned all his virtues to his overthrow,
" And gained our elders to pronounce a foe.
" His right for sums of necessary gold
" Shall first be pawned, and afterwards be sold ;
" Till time shall ever-wanting David draw
" To pass your doubtful title into law.
" If not, the people have a right supreme
 To make their kings, for kings are made for them. 410
' All empire is no more than power in trust,
 Which, when resumed, can be no longer just.
" Succession, for the general good designed,
" In its own wrong a nation cannot bind
" If altering that the people can relieve,
" Better one suffer than a nation grieve.
" The Jews well know their power : ere Saul they chose
" God was their King, and God they durst depose.

" Urge now your piety, your filial name,
" A father's right and fear of future fame,   420
" The public good, that universal call,
" To which even Heaven submitted, answers all.
" Nor let his love enchant your generous mind ;
" 'Tis Nature's trick to propagate her kind.
" Our fond begetters, who would never die,
" Love but themselves in their posterity.
" Or let his kindness by the effects be tried
" Or let him lay his vain pretence aside.
" God said, He loved your father ; could He bring
" A better proof than to anoint him King ?   430
" It surely showed, He loved the shepherd well
" Who gave so fair a flock as Israel.
" Would David have you thought his darling son ?
" What means he then to alienate the crown ?
" The name of godly he may blush to bear ;
" 'Tis after God's own heart to cheat his heir.
" He to his brother gives supreme command,
" To you a legacy of barren land,
" Perhaps the old harp on which he thrums his lays
" Or some dull Hebrew ballad in your praise.   440
" Then the next heir, a prince severe and wise,
" Already looks on you with jealous eyes,
" Sees through the thin disguises of your arts,
" And marks your progress in the people's hearts ;
" Though now his mighty soul its grief contains,
" He meditates revenge who least complains ;
" And like a lion, slumbering in the way
" Or sleep dissembling, while he waits his prey,
" His fearless foes within his distance draws,
" Constrains his roaring and contracts his paws,   450
" Till at the last, his time for fury found,
" He shoots with sudden vengeance from the ground,
" The prostrate vulgar passes o'er and spares,
" But with a lordly rage his hunters tears ;

"Your case no tame expedients will afford,
"Resolve on death or conquest by the sword,
"Which for no less a stake than life you draw,
"And self-defence is Nature's eldest law.
"Leave the warm people no considering time,
"For then rebellion may be thought a crime. 460
"Prevail yourself of what occasion gives,
"But try your title while your father lives ;
"And, that your arms may have a fair pretence,
"Proclaim you take them in the King's defence ;
"Whose sacred life each minute would expose
"To plots from seeming friends and secret foes.
"And who can sound the depth of David's soul ?
"Perhaps his fear his kindness may control :
"He fears his brother, though he loves his son,
"For plighted vows too late to be undone. . . . 470
"Doubt not : but, when he most affects the frown,
"Commit a pleasing rape upon the crown.
"Secure his person to secure your cause
"They, who possess the Prince, possess the laws."

He said, and this advice above the rest
With Absalom's mild nature suited best ;
Unblamed of life (ambition set aside),
Not stained with cruelty nor puffed with pride, 480
How happy had he been, if Destiny
Had higher placed his birth or not so high !
His kingly virtues might have claimed a throne
And blessed all other countries but his own ;
But charming greatness since so few refuse,
'Tis juster to lament him than accuse.
Strong were his hopes a rival to remove,
With blandishments to gain the public love,
To head the faction while their zeal was hot,

B

And popularly prosecute the plot.   490
To further this, Achitophel unites
The malcontents of all the Israelites,
Whose differing parties he could wisely join
For several ends to serve the same design ;
The best, (and of the princes some were such,)
Who thought the power of monarchy too much ;
Mistaken men and patriots in their hearts,
Not wicked, but seduced by impious arts ;
By these the springs of property were bent
And wound so high they cracked the government.   500
The next for interest sought to embroil the state
To sell their duty at a dearer rate,
And make their Jewish markets of the throne ;
Pretending public good to serve their own.
Others thought kings an useless heavy load,
Who cost too much and did too little good.
These were for laying honest David by
On principles.of pure good husbandry.
With them joined all the haranguers of the throng
That thought to get preferment by the tongue.   510
Who follow next a double danger bring,
Not·only hating David, but the King ;
The Solymæan rout, well versed of old
In godly faction and in treason bold,
Cowering and quaking at a conqueror's sword,
But lofty to a lawful prince restored,
Saw with disdain an Ethnic plot begun
And scorned by Jebusites to be outdone.
Hot Levites headed these ; who pulled before
From the ark, which in the Judges' days they bore,   520
Resumed their cant, and with a zealous cry
Pursued their old beloved theocracy,
Where Sanhedrin and priest enslaved the nation
And justified their spoils by inspiration ;
For who so fit for reign as Aaron's race,

If once dominion they could found in grace ?
These led the pack ; though not of surest scent
Yet deepest mouthed against the government.
A numerous host of dreaming saints succeed
Of the true old enthusiastic breed :   530
'Gainst form and order they their power employ
Nothing to build and all things to destroy.
But far more numerous was the herd of such
Who think too little and who talk too much.
These out of mere instinct, they knew not why,
Adored their fathers' God and property,
And by the same blind benefit of Fate
The Devil and the Jebusite did hate :
Born to be saved even in their own despite
Because they could not help believing right.   540
Such were the tools ; but a whole hydra more
Remains of sprouting heads too long to score.
Some of their chiefs were princes of the land ;
In the first rank of these did Zimri stand
A man so various that he seemed to be
Not one, but all mankind's epitome :
Stiff in opinions, always in the wrong,
Was everything by starts and nothing long ;
But in the course of one revolving moon
Was chymist, fiddler, statesman, and buffoon ;   550
Then all for women, painting, rhyming, drinking,
Besides ten thousand freaks that died in thinking.
Blest madman, who could every hour employ
With something new to wish or to enjoy !
Railing and praising were his usual themes,
And both, to show his judgment, in extremes ·
So over violent or over civil
That every man with him was God or Devil.
In squandering wealth was his peculiar art ·
Nothing went unrewarded but desert.   560
Beggared by fools whom still he found too late

He had his jest, and they had his estate.
He laughed himself from Court ; then sought relief
By forming parties, but could ne'er be chief :
For spite of him, the weight of business fell
On Absalom and wise Achitophel ;
Thus wicked but in will, of means bereft,
He left not faction, but of that was left.
   Titles and names 'twere tedious to rehearse
Of lords below the dignity of verse.   570
Wits, warriors, commonwealth's-men were the best ;
Kind husbands and mere nobles all the rest.
And therefore in the name of dulness be
The well-hung Balaam and cold Caleb free ;
And canting Nadab let oblivion damn
Who made new porridge for the paschal lamb.
Let friendship's holy band some names assure,
Some their own worth, and some let scorn secure.
Nor shall the rascal rabble here have place
Whom kings no titles gave, and God no grace :   580
Not bull-faced Jonas, who could statutes draw
To mean rebellion and make treason law.
But he, though bad, is followed by a worse,
The wretch who Heaven's anointed dared to curse ;
Shimei, whose youth did early promise bring
Of zeal to God and hatred to his King,
Did wisely from expensive sins refrain
And never broke the Sabbath but for gain :
Nor ever was he known an oath to vent
Or curse, unless against the government.   590
Thus heaping wealth by the most ready way
Among the Jews, which was to cheat and pray,
The City, to reward his pious hate
Against his master, chose him magistrate.
His hand a vare of justice did uphold,
His neck was loaded with a chain of gold.
During his office treason was no crime,

The 'sons of Belial had a glorious time ;
For Shimei, though not prodigal of pelf,
Yet loved his wicked neighbour as himself,   600
When two or three were gathered to declaim
Against the monarch of Jerusalem,
Shimei was always in the midst of them :
And, if they cursed the King when he was by,
Would rather curse than break good company.
If any durst his factious friends accuse,
He packed a jury of dissenting Jews ;
Whose fellow-feeling in the godly cause
Would free the suffering saint from human laws
For laws are only made to punish those   610
Who serve the King, and to protect his foes.
If any leisure time he had from power,
Because 'tis sin to misemploy an hour,
His business was by writing to persuade
That kings were useless and a clog to trade :
And that his noble style he might refine,
No Rechabite more shunned the fumes of wine.
Chaste were his cellars, and his shrieval board
The grossness of a city feast abhorred :
His cooks with long disuse their trade forgot ;   620
Cool was his kitchen, though his brains were hot.
Such frugal virtue malice may accuse,
But sure 'twas necessary to the Jews :
For towns once burnt such magistrates require
As dare not tempt God's providence by fire.
With spiritual food he fed his servants well,
But free from flesh that made the Jews rebel ·
And Moses' laws he held in more account
For forty days of fasting in the mount.
To speak the rest, who better are forgot,   630
Would tire a well-breathed witness of the plot.
Yet, Corah, thou shalt from oblivion pass ;
Erect thyself, thou monumental brass,

High as the serpent of thy metal made,
While nations stand secure beneath thy shade.
What though his birth were base, yet comets rise
From earthly vapours, ere they shine in skies.
Prodigious actions may as well be done
By weaver's issue as by prince's son.
This arch-attester for the public good   640
By that one deed ennobles all his blood.
Who ever asked the witnesses' high race
Whose oath with martyrdom did Stephen grace ?
Ours was a Levite, and as times went then,
His tribe were God Almighty's gentlemen.
— Sunk were his eyes, his voice was harsh and loud,
Sure signs he neither choleric was nor proud :
His long chin proved his wit, his saint-like grace
A church vermilion and a Moses' face.
His memory, miraculously great,   650
Could plots exceeding man's belief repeat ;
Which therefore cannot be accounted lies.
For human wit could never such devise.
Some future truths are mingled in his book,
But where the witness failed, the prophet spoke.
Some things like visionary flights appear ;
The spirit caught him up, the Lord knows where ;
And gave him his Rabbinical degree
Unknown to foreign University.
His judgment yet his memory did excel,   660
Which pieced his wondrous evidence so well
And suited to the temper of the times,
Then groaning under Jebusitic crimes.
Let Israel's foes suspect his heavenly call
And rashly judge his writ apocryphal ;
Our laws for such affronts have forfeits made,
He takes his life who takes away his trade.
Were I myself in witness Corah's place,
The wretch who did me such a dire disgrace

Should whet my memory, though once forgot,   670
To make him an appendix of my plot.
His zeal to Heaven made him his Prince despise,
And load his person with indignities.
But zeal peculiar privilege affords,
Indulging latitude to deeds and words :
And Corah might for Agag's murder call,
In terms as coarse as Samuel used to Saul.
What others in his evidence did join,
The best that could be had for love or coin,
In Corah's own predicament will fall,   680
For Witness is a common name to all.

Surrounded thus with friends of every sort,
Deluded Absalom forsakes the court ;
Impatient of high hopes, urged with renown,
And fired with near possession of a crown.
The admiring crowd are dazzled with surprise
And on his goodly person feed their eyes.
His joy concealed, he sets himself to show,
On each side bowing popularly low,
His looks, his gestures, and his words he frames   690
And with familiar ease repeats their names.
Thus formed by nature, furnished out with arts,
He glides unfelt into their secret hearts.
Then with a kind compassionating look,
And sighs, bespeaking pity ere he spoke,
Few words he said, but easy those and fit,
More slow than Hybla-drops and far more sweet
    " I mourn, my countrymen, your lost estate,
" Though far unable to prevent your fate :
" Behold a banished man, for your dear cause   700
" Exposed a prey to arbitrary laws !
" Yet oh that I alone could be undone,
" Cut off from empire, and no more a son !
" Now all your liberties a spoil are made,

" Egypt and Tyrus intercept your trade,
" And Jebusites your sacred rites invade.
" My father, whom with reverence yet I name,
" Charmed into ease, is careless of his fame
" And, bribed with petty sums of foreign gold,
" Is grown in Bathsheba's embraces old ;   710
" Exalts his enemies, his friends destroys,
" And all his power against himself employs.
" He gives, and let him give, my right away ;
" But why should he his own and yours betray ?
" He, only he can make the nation bleed,
" And he alone from my revenge is freed.
" Take then my tears (with that he wiped his eyes),
" 'Tis all the aid my present power supplies :
" No court-informer can these arms accuse ;
" These arms may sons against their fathers use.   720
" And 'tis my wish, the next successor's reign
" May make no other Israelite complain."

  Youth, beauty, graceful action seldom fail,
But common interest always will prevail ;
And pity never ceases to be shown
To him who makes the people's wrongs his own.
The crowd that still believe their kings oppress
With lifted hands their young Messiah bless :
Who now begins his progress to ordain
With chariots, horsemen, and a numerous train ;   730
From east to west his glories he displays
And, like the sun, the promised land surveys.
Fame runs before him as the morning star,
And shouts of joy salute him from afar ;
Each house receives him as a guardian god
And consecrates the place of his abode.
But hospitable treats did most commend
Wise Issachar, his wealthy western friend.
This moving court that caught the people's eyes,

And seemed but pomp, did other ends disguise ;   740
Achitophel had formed it, with intent
To sound the depths and fathom, where it went,
The people's hearts, distinguish friends from foes,
And try their strength before they came to blows.
Yet all was coloured with a smooth pretence
Of specious love and duty to their prince.
Religion and redress of grievances,
Two names that always cheat and always please,
Are often urged ; and good king David's life
Endangered by a brother and a wife.   750
Thus in a pageant show a plot is made,
And peace itself is war in masquerade.
Oh foolish Israel ! never warned by ill !
Still the same bait, and circumvented still !
Did ever men forsake their present ease,
In midst of health imagine a disease,
Take pains contingent mischiefs to foresee,
Make heirs for monarchs, and for God decree ?
What shall we think ?   Can people give away
Both for themselves and sons their native sway ?   760
Then they are left defenceless to the sword
Of each unbounded, arbitrary lord ;
And laws are vain by which we right enjoy,
If kings unquestioned can those laws destroy.
Yet if the crowd be judge of fit and just,
And kings are only officers in trust,
Then this resuming covenant was declared
When kings were made, or is for ever barred.
If those who gave the sceptre could not tie
By their own deed their own posterity,   770
How then could Adam bind his future race ?
How could his forfeit on mankind take place ?
Or how could heavenly justice damn us all
Who ne'er consented to our father's fall ?
Then kings are slaves to those whom they command

And tenants to their people's pleasure stand.
Add that the power, for property allowed,
Is mischievously seated in the crowd ;
For who can be secure of private right,
If sovereign sway may be dissolved by might ?   780
Nor is the people's judgment always true
The most may err as grossly as the few,
And faultless kings run down by common cry
For vice, oppression, and for tyranny.
What standard is there in a fickle rout,
Which, flowing to the mark, runs faster out ?
Nor only crowds but Sanhedrins may be
Infected with this public lunacy,
And share the madness of rebellious times,
To murder monarchs for imagined crimes.   790
If they may give and take whene'er they please,
Not kings alone, the Godhead's images,
But government itself at length must fall
To nature's state, where all have right to all.
Yet grant our lords, the people, kings can make,
What prudent men a settled throne would shake ?
For whatsoe'er their sufferings were before,
That change they covet makes them suffer more.
All other errors but disturb a state,
But innovation is the blow of fate.   800
If ancient fabrics nod and threat to fall,
To patch the flaws and buttress up the wall,
Thus far 'tis duty : but here fix the mark ;
For all beyond it is to touch our ark.
To change foundations, cast the frame anew,
Is work for rebels who base ends pursue,
At once divine and human laws control,
And mend the parts by ruin of the whole.
The tampering world is subject to this curse,
To physic their disease into a worse.   810

Now what relief can righteous David bring?
How fatal 'tis to be too good a king!
Friends he has few, so high the madness grows;
Who dare be such must be the people's foes.
Yet some there were even in the worst of days;
Some let me name, and naming is to praise.

In this short file Barzillai first appears,
Barzillai, crowned with honour and with years.
Long since the rising rebels he withstood
In regions waste beyond the Jordan's flood: 820
Unfortunately brave to buoy the state,
But sinking underneath his master's fate.
In exile with his godlike prince he mourned,
For him he suffered, and with him returned.
The court he practised, not the courtier's art:
Large was his wealth, but larger was his heart,
Which well the noblest objects knew to chuse,
The fighting warrior, and recording Muse.
His bed could once a fruitful issue boast;
Now more than half a father's name is lost.   830
His eldest hope, with every grace adorned,
By me, so Heaven will have it, always mourned
And always honoured, snatched in manhood's prime
By unequal fates and Providence's crime:
Yet not before the goal of honour won,
All parts fulfilled of subject and of son;
Swift was the race, but short the time to run.
Oh narrow circle, but of power divine,
Scanted in space, but perfect in thy line!
By sea, by land, thy matchless worth was known,   840
Arms thy delight, and war was all thy own
Thy force infused the fainting Tyrians propped:
And haughty Pharaoh found his fortune stopped.
Oh ancient honour! oh unconquered hand,
Whom foes unpunished never could withstand!

But Israel was unworthy of thy name :
Short is the date of all immoderate fame.
It looks as Heaven our ruin had designed,
And durst not trust thy fortune and thy mind.
Now, free from earth, thy disencumbered soul   850
Mounts up, and leaves behind the clouds and starry pole :
From thence thy kindred legions mayest thou bring
To aid the guardian angel of thy King.
Here stop, my Muse, here cease thy painful flight ;
No pinions can pursue immortal height
Tell good Barzillai thou canst sing no more,
And tell thy soul she should have fled before :
Or fled she with his life, and left this verse
To hang on her departed patron's hearse ?
Now take thy steepy flight from heaven, and see   860
If thou canst find on earth another he :
Another he would be too hard to find ;
See then whom thou canst see not far behind.
Zadoc the priest, whom, shunning power and place,
His lowly mind advanced to David's grace.
With him the Sagan of Jerusalem,
Of hospitable soul and noble stem ;
Him of the western dome, whose weighty sense
Flows in fit words and heavenly eloquence.
The Prophets' sons, by such example led,   870
To learning and to loyalty were bred ·
For colleges on bounteous kings depend
And never rebel was to arts a friend.
To these succeed the pillars of the laws,
Who best could plead. and best can judge a cause.
Next them a train of loyal peers ascend ;
Sharp-judging Adriel, the Muses' friend,
Himself a Muse : in Sanhedrin's debate
True to his Prince, but not a slave of state ;
Whom David's love with honours did adorn   880
That from his disobedient son were torn.

Jotham of piercing wit and pregnant thought,
Endued by nature and by learning taught
To move assemblies, who but only tried
The worse a while, then chose the better side,
Nor chose alone, but turned the balance too,
So much the weight of one brave man can do.
Hushai, the friend of David in distress,
In public storms of manly stedfastness ;
By foreign treaties he informed his youth   890
And joined experience to his native truth.
His frugal care supplied the wanting throne,
Frugal for that, but bounteous of his own :
'Tis easy conduct when exchequers flow,
But hard the task to manage well the low.
For sovereign power is too depressed or high,
When kings are forced to sell or crowds to buy.
Indulge one labour more, my weary Muse,
For Amiel : who can Amiel's praise refuse ?
Of ancient race by birth, but nobler yet   900
In his own worth and without title great :
The Sanhedrin long time as chief he ruled,
Their reason guided and their passion cooled :
So dexterous was he in the Crown's defence,
So formed to speak a loyal nation's sense,
That, as their band was Israel's tribes in small,
So fit was he to represent them all.
Now rasher charioteers the seat ascend,
Whose loose careers his steady skill commend :
They, like the unequal ruler of the day,   910
Misguide the seasons and mistake the way,
While he, withdrawn, at their mad labour smiles
And safe enjoys the sabbath of his toils.

These were the chief, a small but faithful band
Of worthies in the breach who dared to stand
And tempt the united fury of the land.

With grief they viewed such powerful engines bent
To batter down the lawful government.
A numerous faction, with pretended frights
In Sanhedrins to plume the regal rights ;   920
The true successor from the Court removed ;
The plot by hireling witnesses improved.
These ills they saw, and, as their duty bound,
They showed the King the danger of the wound ;
That no concessions from the throne would please,
But lenitives fomented the disease ;
That Absalom, ambitious of the crown,
Was made the lure to draw the people down ;
That false Achitophel's pernicious hate
Had turned the plot to ruin Church and State ;   930
The council violent, the rabble worse ;
That Shimei taught Jerusalem to curse.

    With all these loads of injuries opprest,
And long revolving in his careful breast
The event of things, at last his patience tired,
Thus from his royal throne, by Heaven inspired,
The godlike David spoke ; with awful fear
His train their Maker in their master hear.

    "Thus long have I, by native mercy swayed,
"My wrongs dissembled, my revenge delayed ;   940
"So willing to forgive the offending age ;
"So much the father did the king assuage.
"But now so far my clemency they slight,
"The offenders question my forgiving right.
"That one was made for many, they contend ;
"But 'tis to rule, for that's a monarch's end.
"They call my tenderness of blood my fear,
"Though manly tempers can the longest bear
"Yet since they will divert my native course,
"'Tis time to show I am not good by force.   950

"Those heaped affronts that haughty subjects bring
"Are burdens for a camel, not a king.
"Kings are the public pillars of the State,
"Born to sustain and prop the nation's weight:
"If my young Samson will pretend a call
"To shake the column, let him share the fall;
"But oh that yet he would repent and live!
"How easy 'tis for parents to forgive!
"With how few tears a pardon might be won
"From nature, pleading for a darling son!   960
"Poor pitied youth, by my paternal care
"Raised up to all the height his frame could bear!
"Had God ordained his fate for empire born,
"He would have given his soul another turn
"Gulled with a patriot's name, whose modern sense
"Is one that would by law supplant his prince;
"The people's brave, the politician's tool;
"Never was patriot yet but was a fool.
"Whence comes it that religion and the laws
"Should more be Absalom's than David's cause?   970
"His old instructor, ere he lost his place,
"Was never thought endued with so much grace.
"Good heavens, how faction can a patriot paint!
"My rebel ever proves my people's saint.
"Would they impose an heir upon the throne?
"Let Sanhedrins be taught to give their own.
"A king's at least a part of government,
"And mine as requisite as their consent:
"Without my leave a future king to choose
"Infers a right the present to depose.   980
"True, they petition me to approve their choice·
"But Esau's hands suit ill with Jacob's voice.
"My pious subjects for my safety pray,
"Which to secure, they take my power away.
"From plots and treasons Heaven preserve my years,
"But save me most from my petitioners.

" Unsatiate as the barren womb or grave,

" God cannot grant so much as they can crave.

" What then is left but with a jealous eye

" To guard the small remains of royalty ?   990

" The law shall still direct my peaceful sway,

" And the same law teach rebels to obey :

" Votes shall no more established power control,

" Such votes as make a part exceed the whole.

" No groundless clamours shall my friends remove

" Nor crowds have power to punish ere they prove ;

" For gods and godlike kings their care express

" Still to defend their servants in distress.

" Oh that my power to saving were confined !

" Why am I forced, like Heaven, against my mind 1000

" To make examples of another kind ?

" Must I at length the sword of justice draw ?

" Oh curst effects of necessary law !

" How ill my fear they by my mercy scan !

" Beware the fury of a patient man.

" Law they require, let Law then show her face ;

" They could not be content to look on Grace,

" Her hinder parts, but with a daring eye

" To tempt the terror of her front and die.

" By their own arts, 'tis righteously decreed,   1010

" Those dire artificers of death shall bleed.

" Against themselves their witnesses will swear

" Till, viper-like, their mother-plot they tear,

" And suck for nutriment that bloody gore

" Which was their principle of life before.

" Their Belial with their Beelzebub will fight ;

" Thus on my foes my foes shall do me right.

" Nor doubt the event ; for factious crowds engage

" In their first onset all their brutal rage.

" Then let them take an unresisted course ;   1020

" Retire and traverse, and delude their force :

" But when they stand all breathless, urge the fight

" And rise upon them with redoubled might :
" For lawful power is still superior found,
" When long driven back at length it stands the ground."

He said. The Almighty, nodding, gave consent ;
And peals of thunder shook the firmament.
Henceforth a series of new time began,
The mighty years in long procession ran ;
Once more the godlike David was restored,   1030
And willing nations knew ‘their lawful lord.

THE SECOND PART OF
ABSALOM AND ACHITOPHEL.

A POEM.

"Si quis tamen hæc quoque, si quis
Captus amore leget."
VIRG. *Ecl.* vi. 10.

[*By* NAHUM TATE, *with assistance from* DRYDEN.]

ABSALOM AND ACHITOPHEL.

THE SECOND PART.

Since men, like beasts, each other's prey were made,
Since trade began and priesthood grew a trade,
Since realms were formed, none sure so cursed as those
That madly their own happiness oppose ;
There Heaven itself and godlike kings in vain
Shower down the manna of a gentle reign ;
While pampered crowds to mad sedition run
And monarchs by indulgence are undone.
Thus David's clemency was fatal grown,
While wealthy faction awed the wanting throne.   10
For now their sovereign's orders to contemn
Was held the charter of Jerusalem ;
His rights to invade, his tributes to refuse,
A privilege peculiar to the Jews ;
As if from heavenly call this licence fell
And Jacob's seed were chosen to rebel !

Achitophel with triumph sees his crimes
Thus suited to the madness of the times,
And Absalom, to make his hopes succeed,
Of flattery's charms no longer stands in need,　　　20
While fond of change, though ne'er so dearly bought,
Our tribes outstrip the youth's ambitious thought.
His swiftest hopes with swifter homage meet,
And crowd their servile necks beneath his feet.
Thus to his aid while pressing tides repair,
He mounts and spreads his streamers in the air.
The charms of empire might his youth mislead,
But what can our besotted Israel plead?
Swayed by a monarch, whose serene command
Seems half the blessing of our promised land;　　　30
Whose only grievance is excess of ease,
Freedom our pain, and plenty our disease!
Yet, as all folly would lay claim to sense
And wickedness ne'er wanted a pretence,
With arguments they'd make their treason good
And righteous David's self with slanders load:
That arts of foreign sway he did affect
And guilty Jebusites from law protect,
Whose very chiefs, convict, were never freed,
Nay we have seen their sacrificers bleed!　　　40
Accusers' infamy is urged in vain,
While in the bounds of sense they did contain,
But soon they launched into the unfathomed tide
And in the depths they knew disdained to ride;
For probable discoveries to dispense
Was thought below a pensioned evidence.
Mere truth was dull, nor suited with the port
Of pampered Corah, when advanced to court.
No less than wonders now they will impose
And projects void of grace or sense disclose.　　　50
Such was the charge on pious Michal brought,
Michal, that ne'er was cruel even in thought;

The best of queens and most obedient wife
Impeached of curst designs on David's life!
His life, the theme of her eternal prayer;
'Tis scarce so much his guardian angel's care.
Not summer morns such mildness can disclose,
The Hermon lily nor the Sharon rose.
Neglecting each vain pomp of majesty,
Transported Michal feeds her thoughts on high.   60
She lives with angels and, as angels do,
Quits heaven sometimes to bless the world below,
Where, cherished by her bounty's plenteous spring,
Reviving widows smile and orphans sing.
Oh! when rebellious Israel's crimes at height
Are threatened with her lord's approaching fate,
The piety of Michal then remain
In Heaven's remembrance and prolong his reign.

Less desolation did the pest pursue
That from Dan's limits to Beersheba slew,   70
Less fatal the repeated wars of Tyre,
And less Jerusalem's avenging fire;
With gentler terror these our State o'erran,
Than since our evidencing days began!
On every cheek a pale confusion sat,
Continued fear beyond the worst of fate!
Trust was no more, art, science, useless made
All occupations lost but Corah's trade.
Meanwhile, a guard on modest Corah wait,
If not for safety, needful yet for state.   80
Well might he deem each peer and prince his slave,
And lord it o'er the tribes which he could save:
Even vice in him was virtue; what sad fate
But for his honesty, had seized our State?
And with what tyranny had we been curst,
Had Corah never proved a villain first?
To have told his knowledge of the intrigue in gross

Had been, alas! to our deponent's loss.
The travelled Levite had the experience got
To husband well and make the best of his plot,   90
And therefore, like an evidence of skill,
With wise reserves secured his pension still,
Nor quite of future power himself bereft,
But limbos large for unbelievers left.
For now his writ such reverence had got,
'Twas worse than plotting to suspect his plot.
Some were so well convinced, they made no doubt
Themselves to help the foundered swearers out,
Some had their sense imposed on by their fear,
But more for interest sake believe and swear;   100
E'en to that height with some the frenzy grew,
They raged to find their danger not prove true.

Yet than all these a viler crew remain,
Who with Achitophel the cry maintain;
Not urged by fear, nor through misguided sense,
(Blind zeal and starving need had some pretence;)
But for the good old cause, that did excite
The original rebels' wiles, revenge, and spite,
These raise the plot, to have the scandal thrown
Upon the bright successor of the crown,   110
Whose virtue with such wrongs they had pursued
As seemed all hope of pardon to exclude.
Thus, while on private ends their zeal is built,
The cheated crowd applaud and share their guilt.

Such practices as these, too gross to lie
Long unobserved by each discerning eye,
The more judicious Israelites unspelled,
Though still the charm the giddy rabble held.
Even Absalom amid the dazzling beams
Of empire and ambition's flattering dreams,   120
Perceives the plot too foul to be excused,

To aid designs no less pernicious used;
And, filial sense yet striving in his breast,
Thus to Achitophel his doubts exprest:

" *Why are my thoughts upon a crown employed,*
" *Which once obtained can be but half enjoyed?*
" *Not so, when virtue did my arms require*
" *And to my father's wars I flew entire.*
" *My regal power how will my foes resent,*
" *When I myself have scarce my own consent?*   130
" *Give me a son's unblemished truth again*
" *Or quench the sparks of duty that remain.*
" *How slight to force a throne that legions guard*
" *The task to me; to prove unjust, how hard!*
" *And if the imagined guilt thus wound my thought,*
" *What will it, when the tragic scene is wrought?*
" *Dire war must first be conjured from below,*
" *The realm we'd rule we first must overthrow,*
" *And when the civil Furies are on wing*
" *That blind and undistinguished slaughters fling,*   140
" *Who knows what impious chance may reach the King?*
" *Oh! rather let me perish in the strife,*
" *Than have my crown the price of David's life!*
" *Or if the tempest of the war he stand,*
" *In peace some vile officious villain's hand*
" *His soul's anointed temple may invade,*
" *Or, pressed by clamorous crowds, myself be made*
" *His murderer; rebellious crowds, whose guilt*
" *Shall dread his vengeance till his blood be spilt;*
" *Which if my filial tenderness oppose,*   150
" *Since to the empire by their arms I rose,*
" *Those very arms on me shall be employed,*
" *A new usurper crowned and I destroyed.*
" *The same pretence of public good will hold*
" *And new Achitophels be found as bold*
" *To urge the needful change, perhaps the old.*"

He said.   The statesman with a smile replies,
A smile that did his rising spleen disguise:
" *My thoughts presumed our labours at an end,*
" *And are we still with conscience to contend ?*   160
" *Whose want in kings as needful is allowed*
" *As 'tis for them to find it in the crowd.*
" *Far in the doubtful passage you are gone,*
" *And only can be safe by pressing on.*
" *The crown's true heir, a prince severe and wise,*
" *Has viewed your motions long with jealous eyes,*
" *Your person's charms, your more prevailing arts,*
" *And marked your progress in the people's hearts ,*
" *Whose patience is the effect of stinted power,*
" *But treasures vengeance for the fatal hour ;*   170
" *And if remote the peril he can bring.*
" *Your present danger's greater from the King.*
" *Let not a parent's name deceive your sense,*
" *Nor trust the father in a jealous Prince!*
" *Your trivial faults if he could so resent*
" *To doom you little less than banishment,*
" *What rage must your presumption since inspire,*
" *Against his orders your return from Tyre ?*
" *Nor only so, but with a pomp more high*
" *And open court of popularity,*   180
" *The factious tribes*"—" *And this reproof from thee!* "
The Prince replies, "O statesman's winding skill,
" *They first condemn that first advised the ill!* "
" *Illustrious youth," returned Achitophel,*
" *Miscontrue not the words that mean you well.*
" *The course you steer I worthy blame conclude,*
" *But 'tis because you leave it unpursued.*
" *A monarch's crown with fate surrounded lies,*
" *Who reach lay hold on death that miss the prize.*
" *Did you for this expose yourself to show*   190
" *And to the crowd bow popularly low,*
" *For this your glorious progress next ordain,*

" *With chariots, horsemen, and a numerous train,*
" *With fame before you like the morning star,*
" *And shouts of joy saluting from afar?*
" *Oh, from the heights you've reached but take a view,*
" *Scarce leading Lucifer could fall like you!*
" *And must I here my shipwracked arts bemoan?*
" *Have I for this so oft made Israel groan,*
" *Your single interest with the nation weighed,*   200
" *And turned the scale where your desires were laid,*
" *Even when at helm a course so dangerous moved,*
" *To land your hopes, as my removal proved?* "

     " *I not dispute,*" *the royal youth replies,*
" *The known perfection of your policies;*
" *Nor in Achitophel yet grudge or blame*
" *The privilege that statesmen ever claim,*
" *Who private interest never yet pursued,*
" *But still pretended 'twas for others' good.*
" *What politician yet e'er scaped his fate*   210
" *Who, saving his own neck, not saved the State?*
" *From hence on every humourous wind that veered*
" *With shifted sails a several course you steered.*
" *What form of sway did David e'er pursue*
" *That seemed like absolute, but sprung from you?*
" *Who at your instance quashed each penal law*
" *That kept dissenting factious Jews in awe;*
" *And who suspends fixed laws may abrogate,*
" *That done, form new, and so enslave the state.*
" *Even property, whose champion now you stand,*   220
" *And seem for this the idol of the land,*
" *Did ne'er sustain such violence before*
" *As when your counsel shut the royal store,*
" *Advice that ruin to whole tribes procured,*
" *But secret kept till your own banks secured.*
" *Recount with this the triple covenant broke,*
" *And Israel fitted for a foreign yoke;*

" *Nor here your counsels' fatal progress stayed,*
" *But sent our levied powers to Pharaoh's aid;*
" *Hence Tyre and Israel, low in ruins laid,*   230
" *And Egypt, once their scorn, their common terror made.*
" *Even yet of such a season we can dream,*
" *When royal rights you made your darling theme,*
" *For power unlimited could reasons draw*
" *And place prerogative above the law;*
" *Which on your fall from office grew unjust,*
" *The laws made king, the king a slave in trust:*
" *Whom with state-craft, to interest only true,*
" *You now accuse of ills contrived by you.*"

     To this Hell's agent—" *Royal youth, fix here,*   240
" *Let interest be the star by which I steer:*
" *Hence, to repose your trust in me was wise,*
" *Whose interest most in your advancement lies;*
" *A tie so firm as always will avail*
" *When friendship, nature, and religion fail.*
" *On ours the safety of the crowd depends,*
" *Secure the crowd, and we obtain our ends,*
" *Whom I will cause so far our guilt to share,*
" *Till they are made our champions by their fear.*
" *What opposition can your rival bring,*   250
" *While Sanhedrims are jealous of the King?*
" *His strength as yet in David's friendship lies,*
" *And what can David's self without supplies?*
" *Who with exclusive bills must now dispense,*
" *Debar the heir or starve in his defence;*
" *Conditions which our elders ne'er will quit*
" *And David's justice never can admit.*
" *Or forced by wants his brother to betray,*
" *To your ambition next he clears the way,*
" *For if succession once to nought they bring,*   260
" *Their next advance removes the present King:*
" *Persisting else his senates to dissolve*

" *In equal hazard shall his reign involve.*
" *Our tribes, whom Pharaoh's power so much alarms,*
" *Shall rise without their Prince to oppose his arms.*
" *Nor boots it on what cause at first they join,*
" *Their troops, once up, are tools for our design.*
" *At least such subtle covenants shall be made,*
" *Till peace itself is war in masquerade.*
" *Associations of mysterious sense,*   270
" *Against, but seeming for, the King's defence,*
" *Even on their courts of justice fetters draw*
" *And from our agents muzzle up their law.*
" *By which a conquest if we fail to make,*
" *'Tis a drawn game at worst, and we secure our stake.*"

He said, and for the dire success depends
On various sects, by common guilt made friends;
Whose heads, though ne'er so differing in their creed,
In the point of treason yet were well agreed.
'Mongst these, extorting Ishban first appears,   280
Pursued by a meagre troop of bankrupt heirs.
Blest times when Ishban, he whose occupation
So long has been to cheat, reforms the nation!
Ishban of conscience suited to his trade,
As good a saint as usurer ever made.
Yet Mammon has not so engrossed him quite
But Belial lays as large a claim of spite,
Who for those pardons from his Prince he draws
Returns reproaches, and cries up the cause.
That year in which the City he did sway,   290
He left rebellion in a hopeful way;
Yet his ambition once was found so bold
To offer talents of extorted gold,
Could David's wants have so been bribed to shame
And scandalize our peerage with his name;
For which his dear sedition he'd forswear,
And e'en turn loyal, to be made a peer.

Next him, let railing Rabsheka have place,
So full of zeal he has no need of grace ; . . .   300
What caution could appear too much in him
That keeps the treasure of Jerusalem !
Let David's brother but approach the town,
" Double our guards," he cries, " we are undone ! "
Protesting that he dares not sleep in his bed,
" Lest he should rise next morn without his head."

Next these, a troop of busy spirits press,   310
Of little fortunes and of conscience less ;
With them the tribe, whose luxury had drained
Their banks, in former sequestrations gained ;
Who rich and great by past rebellions grew,
And long to fish the troubled waves anew.
Some future hopes, some present payment draws
To sell their conscience and espouse the cause ;
Such stipends those vile hirelings best befit,
Priests without grace and poets without wit.
Shall that false Hebronite escape our curse,   320
Judas, that keeps the rebels' pension-purse,
Judas, that pays the treason-writer's fee,
Judas, that well deserves his namesake's tree,
Who at Jerusalem's own gates erects
His college for a nursery of sects,
Young prophets with an early care secures,
And with the dung of his own arts manures ?
What have the men of Hebron here to do ?
What part in Israel's promised land have you ?
Here Phaleg, the lay Hebronite, is come,   330
'Cause like the rest he could not live at home ;
Who from his own possessions could not drain

An omer even of Hebronitish grain,
Here struts it like a patriot, and talks high
Of injured subjects, altered property :
An emblem of that buzzing insect just
That mounts the wheel, and thinks she raises dust.   . .
A waiting-man to travelling nobles chose,   342
He his own laws would saucily impose,
Till bastinadoed back again he went
To learn those manners he to teach was sent.
Chastised he ought to have retreated home,
But he reads politics to Absalom ;
For never Hebronite, though kicked and scorned,
To his own country willingly returned.

But leaving famished Phaleg to be fed   350
And to talk treason for his daily bread,
Let Hebron, nay let Hell, produce a man
So made for mischief as Ben Jochanan ;
A Jew of humble parentage was he,
By trade a Levite, though of low degree :
His pride no higher than the desk aspired,
But for the drudgery of priests was hired
To read and pray in linen ephod brave
And pick up single shekels from the grave.
Married at last, and finding charge come faster,   360
He could not live by God, but changed his master ·
Inspired by want, was made a factious tool,
They got a villain, and we lost a fool.
Still violent, whatever cause he took,
But most against the party he forsook :
For renegadoes, who ne'er turn by halves,
Are bound in conscience to be double knaves.
So this prose prophet took most monstrous pains

To let his masters see he earned his gains.
But as the Devil owes all his imps a shame,   370
He chose the Apostate for his proper theme ;
With little pains he made the picture true,
And from reflection took the rogue he drew.
A wondrous work, to prove the Jewish nation
In every age a murmuring generation,
To trace them from their infancy of sinning,
And show them factious from their first beginning,
To prove they could rebel, and rail, and mock,
Much to the credit of the chosen flock ;
A strong authority which must convince,   380
That saints own no allegiance to their prince ; . .
But tell me, did the drunken patriarch bless
The son that showed his father's nakedness ?
Such thanks the present Church thy pen will give,
Which proves rebellion was so primitive.
Must ancient failings be examples made ?
Then murderers from Cain may learn their trade.
As thou the heathen and the saint hast drawn,   390
Methinks the Apostate was the better man,
And thy hot father, waving my respect,
Not of a mother church but of a sect.
And such he needs must be of thy inditing,
This comes of drinking asses' milk and writing.
If Balak should be called to leave his place,
(As profit is the loudest call of grace,)
His temple, dispossessed of one, would be
Replenished with seven devils more by thee.

Levi thou art a load, I'll lay thee down,   400
And show rebellion bare, without a gown ·
Poor slaves in metre, dull and addle-pated,
Who rhyme below even David's psalms translated ;

Some in my speedy pace I must outrun,
As lame Mephibosheth the wizard's son ;
To make quick way I'll leap o'er heavy blocks,
Shun rotten Uzza as I would the pox ;
And hasten Og and Doeg to rehearse,
Two fools that crutch their feeble sense on verse,
Who by my Muse to all succeeding times   410
Shall live in spite of their own dogrel rhymes.

Doeg, though without knowing how or why,
Made still a blundering kind of melody ;
Spurred boldly on, and dashed through thick and thin.
Through sense and nonsense, never out nor in ;
Free from all meaning, whether good or bad,
And, in one word, heroically mad,
He was too warm on picking-work to dwell
But faggoted his notions as they fell,
And, if they rhymed and rattled, all was well.   420
Spiteful he is not, though he wrote a satire,
For still there goes some thinking to ill-nature ;
He needs no more than birds and beasts to think,
All his occasions are to eat and drink.
If he call rogue and rascal from a garret,
He means you no more mischief than a parrot ;
The words for friend and foe alike were made,
To fetter them in verse is all his trade. . . .
Let him be gallows-free by my consent, —   431
And nothing suffer, since he nothing meant ;
Hanging supposes human soul and reason,
This animal's below committing treason :
Shall he be hanged who never could rebel ?
That's a preferment for Achitophel. . . .

Railing in other men may be a crime, 441
But ought to pass for mere instinct in him ;
Instinct he follows and no farther knows,
For to write verse with him is to *transprose ;*
'Twere pity treason at his door to lay
Who makes heaven's gate a lock to its own key ;
Let him rail on, let his invective Muse
Have four and twenty letters to abuse,
Which if he jumbles to one line of sense,
Indict him of a capital offence. 450
In fire-works give him leave to vent his spite,
Those are the only serpents he can write ;
The height of his ambition is, we know,
But to be master of a puppet-show ;
On that one stage his works may yet appear,
And a month's harvest keeps him all the year.

Now stop your noses, readers, all and some,
For here's a tun of midnight work to come,
Og from a treason-tavern rolling home.
Round as a globe, and liquored every chink, 460
Goodly and great he sails behind his link.
With all this bulk there's nothing lost in Og,
For every inch that is not fool is rogue : . . . .
When wine has given him courage to blaspheme,
He curses God, but God before cursed him ;
And if man could have reason, none has more,
That made his paunch so rich and him so poor.
With wealth he was not trusted, for Heaven knew 470
What 'twas of old to pamper up a Jew ;
To what would he on quail and pheasant swell
That even on tripe and carrion could rebel ?
But though Heaven made him poor, with reverence
   speaking,

He never was a poet of God's making ;
The midwife laid her hand on his thick skull,
With this prophetic blessing—*Be thou dull*,
Drink, swear, and roar, forbear no lewd delight
Fit for thy bulk, do anything but write.
Thou art of lasting make, like thoughtless men,   480
A strong nativity—but for the pen ;
Eat opium, mingle arsenic in thy drink,
Still thou mayest live, avoiding pen and ink.
I see, I see, 'tis counsel given in vain,
For treason, botched in rhyme, will be thy bane ;
Rhyme is the rock on which thou art to wreck,
'Tis fatal to thy fame and to thy neck.
Why should thy metre good king David blast ?
A psalm of his will surely be thy last.
Darest thou presume in verse to meet thy foes.   490
Thou whom the penny pamphlet foiled in prose ?
Doeg, whom God for mankind's mirth has made,
O'ertops thy talent in thy very trade ;
Doeg to thee, thy paintings are so coarse,
A poet is, though he's the poet's horse.
A double noose thou on thy neck dost pull
For writing treason and for writing dull ;
To die for faction is a common evil,
But to be hanged for nonsense is the devil.
Hadst thou the glories of thy King exprest,   500
Thy praises had been satires at the best ;
But thou in clumsy verse, unlicked, unpointed,
Hast shamefully defied the Lord's anointed :
I will not rake the dunghill of thy crimes,
For who would read thy life that reads thy rhymes ?
But of king David's foes be this the doom,
May all be like the young man Absalom ,
And for my foes may this their blessing be,
To talk like Doeg and to write like thee.

Achitophel each rank, degree, and age   510
For various ends neglects not to engage,
The wise and rich for purse and counsel brought,
The fools and beggars for their number sought,
Who yet not only on the town depends,
For even in court the faction had its friends.
These thought the places they possessed too small,
And in their hearts wished court and king to fall:
Whose names the Muse, disdaining, holds in the dark,
Thrust in the villain herd without a mark
With parasites and libel-spawning imps,   520
Intriguing fops, dull jesters, and worse pimps.
Disdain the rascal rabble to pursue,
Their set cabals are yet a viler crew.
See where involved in common smoke they sit,
Some for our mirth, some for our satire fit;
These gloomy, thoughtful, and on mischief bent,
While those for mere good fellowship frequent
The appointed club, can let sedition pass,
Sense, nonsense, anything to employ the glass,
And who believe in their dull honest hearts,   530
The rest talk treason but to show their parts,
Who ne'er had wit or will for mischief yet,
But pleased to be reputed of a set.

But in the sacred annals of our plot,
Industrious Arod never be forgot:
The labours of this midnight-magistrate
May vie with Corah's to preserve the State.
In search of arms he failed not to lay hold
On war's most powerful dangerous weapon, gold.
And last, to take from Jebusites all odds,   540
Their altars pillaged, stole their very gods.
Oft would he cry, when treasure he surprised,
'Tis Baalish gold in David's coin disguised;
Which to his house with richer relicts came

While lumber idols only fed the flame:
For our wise rabble ne'er took pains to inquire,
What 'twas he burnt, so it made a rousing fire,
With which our elder was enriched no more
Than false Gehazi with the Syrian's store;
So poor, that when our choosing tribes were met,   550
Even for his stinking votes he ran in debt;
For meat the wicked and, as authors think,
The saints he choused for his electing drink;
Thus every shift and subtle method past,
And all to be no Zaken at the last.

Now, raised on Tyre's sad ruins, Pharaoh's pride
Soared high, his legions threatening far and wide;
As when a battering storm engendered high,
By winds upheld, hangs hovering in the sky,
Is gazed upon by every trembling swain,   560
This for his vineyard fears, and that his grain,
For blooming plants and flowers new opening these,
For lambs eaned lately and far-labouring bees,
To guard his stock each to the gods does call,
Uncertain where the fire-charged clouds will fall,
Even so the doubtful nations watch his arms,
With terror each expecting his alarms.
Where, Judah, where was now thy lion's roar?
Thou only couldst the captive lands restore,
But thou, with inbred broils and faction prest,   570
From Egypt needst a guardian with the rest.
Thy Prince from Sanhedrims no trust allowed,
Too much the representers of the crowd,
Who for their own defence give no supply
But what the Crown's prerogatives must buy;
As if their Monarch's rights to violate
More needful were than to preserve the State!
From present dangers they divert their care,
And all their fears are of the royal heir,

Whom now the reigning malice of his foes 580
Unjudged would sentence and ere crowned depose:
Religion the pretence, but their decree
To bar his reign, whate'er his faith shall be.
By Sanhedrims and clamorous crowds thus prest,
What passions rent the righteous David's breast?
Who knows not how to oppose or to comply,
Unjust to grant and dangerous to deny!
How near in this dark juncture Israel's fate,
Whose peace one sole expedient could create,
Which yet the extremest virtue did require 590
Even of that Prince whose downfall they conspire?
His absence David does with tears advise,
To appease their rage; undaunted he complies.
Thus he who, prodigal of blood and ease,
A royal life exposed to winds and seas,
At once contending with the waves and fire,
And heading danger in the wars of Tyre,
Inglorious now forsakes his native sand
And, like an exile, quits the promised land.
Our Monarch scarce from pressing tears refrains, 600
And painfully his royal state maintains.
Who, now embracing on the extremest shore,
Almost revokes what he enjoined before:
Concludes at last more trust to be allowed
To storms and seas than to the raging crowd.
Forbear, rash Muse, the parting scene to draw,
With silence charmed as deep as theirs that saw!
Not only our attending nobles weep,
But hardy sailors swell with tears the deep;
The tide restrained her course, and more amazed 610
The twin-stars on the royal brothers gazed;
While this sole fear——
Does trouble to our suffering hero bring,
Lest next the popular rage oppress the King.
Thus parting, each for the other's danger grieved

The shore the King, and seas the Prince received.
Go, injured hero, while propitious gales,
Soft as thy consort's breath, inspire thy sails.
Well may she trust her beauties on a flood
Where thy triumphant fleets so oft have rode.   620
Safe on thy breast reclined, her rest be deep,
Rocked like a Nereid by the waves asleep;
While happiest dreams her fancy entertain,
And to Elysian fields convert the main!
Go, injured hero, while the shores of Tyre
At thy approach so silent shall admire;
Who on thy thunder still their thoughts employ
And greet thy landing with a trembling joy.

On heroes thus the prophet's fate is thrown,
Admired by every nation but their own;   630
Yet while our factious Jews his worth deny,
Their aching conscience gives their tongue the lie.
Even in the worst of men the noblest parts
Confess him, and he triumphs in their hearts,
Whom to his King the best respects commend
Of subject, soldier, kinsman, prince and friend;
All sacred names of most divine esteem,
And to perfection all sustained by him;
Wise, just, and constant, courtly without art,
Swift to discern and to reward desert;   640
No hour of his in fruitless ease destroyed,
But on the noblest subjects still employed;
Whose steady soul ne'er learnt to separate
Between his Monarch's interest and the State,
But heaps those blessings on the royal head,
Which he well knows must be on subjects shed.

On what pretence could then the vulgar rage
Against his worth, and native rights engage?
Religious fears their argument are made,

Religious fears his sacred rights invade!   650
Of future superstition they complain
And Jebusitic worship in his reign,
With such alarms his foes the crowd deceive,
With dangers fright which not themselves believe.

Since nothing can our sacred rites remove,
Whate'er the faith of the successor prove,
Our Jews their ark shall undisturbed retain,
At least while their religion is their gain,
Who know by old experience Baal's commands
Not only claimed their conscience but their lands,   660
They grudge God's tithes, how therefore shall they yield
An idol full possession of the field?
Grant such a Prince enthroned, we must confess
The people's sufferings than that monarch's less,
Who must to hard conditions still be bound
And for his quiet with the crowd compound;
Or should his thoughts to tyranny incline,
Where are the means to compass the design?
Our Crown's revenues are too short a store,
And jealous Sanhedrims would give no more.   670

As vain our fears of Egypt's potent aid;
Not so has Pharaoh learnt ambition's trade,
Nor ever with such measures can comply
As shock the common rules of policy.
None dread like him the growth of Israel's king,
And he alone sufficient aids can bring,
Who knows that prince to Egypt can give law
That on our stubborn tribes his yoke could draw.
At such profound expense he has not stood,
Nor dyed for this his hands so deep in blood;   680
Would ne'er through wrong and right his progress take,
Grudge his own rest, and keep the world awake,
To fix a lawless prince on Judah's throne,

First to invade our rights, and then his own;
His dear-gained conquests cheaply to despoil,
And reap the harvest of his crimes and toil.
We grant his wealth vast as our ocean's sand
And curse its fatal influence on our land,
Which our bribed Jews so numerously partake
That even an host his pensioners would make.   690
From these deceivers our divisions spring,
Our weakness and the growth of Egypt's king:
These with pretended friendship to the State
Our crowd's suspicion of their Prince create,
Both pleased and frightened with the specious cry,
To guard their sacred rights and property;
To ruin thus the chosen flock are sold,
While wolves are ta'en for guardians of the fold;
Seduced by these we groundlessly complain,
And loathe the manna of a gentle reign: 700
Thus our forefathers' crooked paths are trod,
We trust our Prince no more than they their God.
But all in vain our reasoning prophets preach
To those whom sad experience ne'er could teach,
Who can commence new broils in bleeding scars
And fresh remembrance of intestine wars;
When the same household mortal foes did yield,
And brothers stained with brothers' blood the field,
When sons' curst steel the fathers' gore did stain,
And mothers mourned for sons by fathers slain!   710
When thick as Egypt's locusts on the sand
Our tribes lay slaughtered through the promised land.
Whose few survivors with worse fate remain,
To drag the bondage of a tyrant's reign;
Which scene of woes unknowing we renew,
And madly even those ills we fear pursue,
While Pharaoh laughs at our domestic broils
And safely crowds his tents with nations' spoils.
Yet our fierce Sanhedrim in restless rage

Against our absent hero still engage,   720
And chiefly urge, such did their frenzy prove,
The only suit their prince forbids to move;
Which till obtained, they cease affairs of state,
And real dangers wave for groundless hate.
Long David's patience waits relief to bring
With all the indulgence of a lawful king,
Expecting till the troubled waves would cease,
But found the raging billows still increase.
The crowd, whose insolence forbearance swells,
While he forgives too far, almost rebels.   730
At last his deep resentments silence broke,
The imperial palace shook, while thus he spoke:

" Then Justice wake, and Rigour take her time,
" For lo! our mercy is become our crime.
" While halting punishment her stroke delays,
" Our sovereign right, Heaven's sacred trust, decays!
" For whose support even subjects' interest calls,
" Woe to that kingdom where the monarch falls!
" That prince who yields the least of regal sway
" So far his people's freedom does betray.   740
" Right lives by law, and law subsists by power;
" Disarm the shepherd, wolves the flock devour.
" Hard lot of empire o'er a stubborn race,
" Which Heaven itself in vain has tried with grace!
" When will our reason's long-charmed eyes unclose,
" And Israel judge between her friends and foes?
" When shall we see expired deceivers' sway,
" And credit what our God and monarchs say?
" Dissembled patriots bribed with Egypt's gold
" Even Sanhedrims in blind obedience hold;   750
" Those patriots' falsehood in their actions see
" And judge by the pernicious fruit the tree;
" If aught for which so loudly they declaim,
" Religion, laws, and freedom, were their aim,

" *Our senates in due methods they had led,*
" *To avoid those mischiefs which they seemed to dread;*
" *But first, ere yet they propped the sinking State,*
" *To impeach and charge, as urged by private hate,*
" *Proves that they ne'er believed the fears they prest,*
" *But barbarously destroyed the nation's rest.*   760
" *Oh! whither will ungoverned senates drive,*
" *And to what bounds licentious votes arrive?*
" *When their injustice we are pressed to share,*
" *The monarch urged to exclude the lawful heir;*
" *Are princes thus distinguished from the crowd,*
" *And this the privilege of royal blood?*
" *But grant we should confirm the wrongs they press,*
" *His sufferings yet were than the people's less;*
" *Condemned for life the murdering sword to wield,*
" *And on their heirs entail a bloody field.*   770
" *Thus madly their own freedom they betray*
" *And for the oppression which they fear make way,*
" *Succession fixed by Heaven, the kingdom's bar,*
" *Which, once dissolved, admits the flood of war;*
" *Waste, rapine, spoil, without the assault begin*
" *And our mad tribes supplant the fence within.*
" *Since, then, their good they will not understand,*
" *'Tis time to take the monarch's power in hand;*
" *Authority and force to join with skill*
" *And save the lunatics against their will.*   780
" *The same rough means that suage the crowd appease*
" *Our senates, raging with the crowd's disease.*
" *Henceforth unbiassed measures let them draw*
" *From no false gloss, but genuine text of law;*
" *Nor urge those crimes upon religion's score*
" *Themselves so much in Jebusites abhor.*
" *Whom laws convict, and only they, shall bleed,*
" *Nor Pharisees by Pharisees be freed.*
" *Impartial justice from our throne shall shower,*
" *All shall have right, and we our sovereign power.*"   790

He said; the attendants heard with awful joy
And glad presages their fixed thoughts employ,
From Hebron now the suffering heir returned,
A realm that long with civil discord mourned,
Till his approach, like some arriving God,
Composed and healed the place of his abode,
The deluge checked that to Judæa spread,
And stopped sedition at the fountain's head.
Thus in forgiving David's paths he drives
And, chased from Israel, Israel's peace contrives.   800
The field confessed his power in arms before,
And seas proclaimed his triumphs to the shore;
As nobly has his sway in Hebron shown,
How fit to inherit godlike David's throne.
Through Sion's streets his glad arrival's spread
And conscious faction shrinks her snaky head;
His train their sufferings think o'erpaid to see
The crowd's applause with virtue once agree.
Success charms all, but zeal for worth distrest,
A virtue proper to the brave and best;   810
'Mongst whom was Jothran, Jothran always bent
To serve the Crown, and loyal by descent;
Whose constancy so firm and conduct just
Deserved at once two royal masters' trust;
Who Tyre's proud arms had manfully withstood
On seas, and gathered laurels from the flood;
Of learning yet no portion was denied,
Friend to the Muses and the Muses' pride.
Nor can Benaiah's worth forgotten lie,
Of steady soul when public storms were high;   820
Whose conduct while the Moor fierce onsets made
Secured at once our honour and our trade.
Such were the chiefs who most his sufferings mourned,
And viewed with silent joy the prince returned,
While those that sought his absence to betray
Press first their nauseous false respects to pay;

Him still the officious hypocrites molest
And with malicious duty break his rest.
While real transports thus his friends employ,
And foes are loud in their dissembled joy,   830
His triumphs, so resounded far and near,
Missed not his young ambitious rival's ear;
And as, when joyful hunters' clamorous train
Some slumbering lion wakes in Moab's plain,
Who oft had forced the bold assailants yield,
And scattered his pursuers through the field,
Disdaining furls his mane and tears the ground,
His eyes inflaming all the desert round,
With roar of seas directs his chasers' way,
Provokes from far and dares them to the fray,   840
Such rage stormed now in Absalom's fierce breast,
Such indignation his fired eyes confest.
Where now was the instructor of his pride?
Slept the old pilot in so rough a tide,
Whose wiles had from the happy shore betrayed,
And thus on shelves the credulous youth conveyed?
In deep revolving thoughts he weighs his state,
Secure of craft, nor doubts to baffle fate;
At least, if his stormed bark must go adrift,
To baulk his charge and for himself to shift,   850
In which his dexterous wit had oft been shown,
And in the wreck of kingdoms saved his own;
But now with more than common danger prest,
Of various resolutions stands possest,
Perceives the crowd's unstable zeal decay,
Lest their recanting chief the cause betray,
Who on a father's grace his hopes may ground
And for his pardon with their heads compound.
Him, therefore, ere his fortune slip her time,
The statesman plots to engage in some bold crime   860
Past pardon; whether to attempt his bed,
Or threat with open arms the royal head;

Or other daring method and unjust
That may confirm him in the people's trust.
But, failing thus to ensnare him, nor secure
How long his foiled ambition may endure,
Plots next to lay him by as past his date,
And try some new pretender's luckier fate ;
Whose hopes with equal toil he would pursue,
Nor cares what claimer's crowned, except the true.   870
Wake, Absalom, approaching ruin shun,
And see, oh see, for whom thou art undone !
How are thy honours and thy fame betrayed,
The property of desperate villains made !
Lost power and conscious fears their crimes create
And guilt in them was little less than fate ;
But why shouldst thou, from every grievance free,
Forsake thy vineyards for their stormy sea ?
For thee did Canaan's milk and honey flow,
Love dressed thy bowers and laurels sought thy brow,   880
Preferment, wealth, and power thy vassals were,
And of a monarch all things but the care :
Oh, should our crimes again that curse draw down,
And rebel arms once more attempt the crown,
Sure ruin waits unhappy Absalon,
Alike by conquest or defeat undone.
Who could relentless see such youth and charms
Expire with wretched fate in impious arms,
A prince so formed, with earth's and Heaven's applause,
To triumph o'er crowned heads in David's cause !   890
Or grant him victor, still his hopes must fail
Who conquering would not for himself prevail ;
The faction whom he trusts for future sway
Him and the public would alike betray ;
Amongst themselves divide the captive State
And found their hydra empire in his fate !
Thus having beat the clouds with painful flight,
The pitied youth with sceptres in his sight,

(So have their cruel politics decreed,)
Must by that crew that made him guilty bleed.   900
For, could their pride brook any prince's sway,
Whom but mild David would they choose to obey ?
Who once at such a gentle reign repine
The fall of monarchy itself design:
From hate to that their reformations spring,
And David not their grievance, but the King.
Seized now with panic fear the faction lies,
Lest this clear truth strike Absalom's charmed eyes;
Lest he perceive, from long enchantment free,
What all beside the flattered youth must see.   910
But whate'er doubts his troubled bosom swell,
Fair carriage still became Achitophel;
Who now an envious festival instals
And to survey their strength the faction calls,
Which fraud, religious worship too, must gild;
But oh how weakly does sedition build!
For, lo! the royal mandate issues forth,
Dashing at once their treason, zeal, and mirth.
So have I seen disastrous chance invade,
Where careful emmets had their forage laid;   920
(Whether fierce Vulcan's rage the furzy plain
Had seized, engendered by some careless swain,
Or swelling Neptune lawless inroads made
And to their cell of store his flood conveyed;)
The commonwealth, broke up, distracted go
And in wild haste their loaded mates o'erthrow:
Even so our scattered guests confusedly meet,
With boiled, baked, roast, all justling in the street,
Dejected all, and ruefully dismayed,
For shekel, without treat or treason, paid.   930

Sedition's dark eclipse now fainter shows,
More bright each hour the royal planet grows,
Of force the clouds of envy to disperse

In kind conjunction of assisting stars
Here, labouring Muse! those glorious chiefs relate
That turned the doubtful scale of David's fate;
The rest of that illustrious band rehearse,
Immortalized in laurelled Asaph's verse.
Hard task! yet will not I thy flight recall;
View heaven, and then enjoy thy glorious fall.　　　　940
　　First, write Bezaliel, whose illustrious name
Forestals our praise, and gives his poet fame
The Kenites' rocky province his command,
A barren limb of fertile Canaan's land;
Which for its generous natives yet could be
Held worthy such a President as he.
Bezaliel with each grace and virtue fraught,
Serene his looks, serene his life and thought;
On whom so largely Nature heaped her store,
There scarce remained for arts to give him more.　　　950
To aid the Crown and State his greatest zeal,
His second care that service to conceal;
Of dues observant, firm in every trust,
And to the needy always more than just;
Who truth from specious falsehood can divide,
Has all the gownsmen's skill without their pride;
Thus, crowned with worth from heights of honour won,
See all his glories copied in his son,
Whose forward fame should every Muse engage,
Whose youth boasts skill denied to others' age.　　　960
Men, manners, language, books of noblest kind,
Already are the conquest of his mind.
Whose loyalty before its date was prime,
Nor waited the dull course of rolling time.
The monster faction early he dismayed,
And David's cause long since confessed his aid.
　　Brave Abdael o'er the Prophets' school was placed;
Abdael, with all his father's virtue graced;
A hero who, while stars looked wondering down,

Without one Hebrew's blood restored the crown.   970
That praise was his; what therefore did remain
For following chiefs but boldly to maintain
That crown restored ?   And in this rank of fame
Brave Abdael with the first a place must claim.
Proceed, illustrious happy chief, proceed,
Foreseize the garlands for thy brow decreed,
While the inspired tribe attend with noblest strain
To register the glories thou shalt gain :
For sure the dew shall Gilboah's hills forsake
And Jordan mix. his stream with Sodom's lake,   980
Or seas retired their secret stores disclose
And to the sun their scaly brood expose,
Or swelled above the cliffs their billows raise,
Before the Muses leave their patron's praise.
Eliab our next labour does invite,
And hard the task to do Eliab right.
Long with the royal wanderer he roved
And firm in all the turns of fortune proved.
Such ancient service and desert so large
Well claimed the royal household for his charge.   990
His age with only one mild heiress blest,
In all the bloom of smiling nature drest;
And blest again to see his flower allied
To David's stock, and made young Othniel's bride !
The bright restorer of his father's youth,
Devoted to a son's and subject's truth :
Resolved to bear that prize of duty home,
So bravely sought, while sought by Absalom.
Ah, Prince ! the illustrious planet of thy birth
And thy more powerful virtue guard thy worth,   1000
May no Achitophel thy ruin boast !
Israel too much in one such wreck has lost.
Even envy must consent to Helon's worth,
Whose soul, though Egypt glories in his birth,
Could for our captive ark its zeal retain

And Pharaoh's altars in their pomp disdain:
To slight his gods was small; with nobler pride
He all the allurements of his court defied.
Whom profit nor example could betray,
But Israel's friend, and true to David's sway. 1010
What acts of favour in his province fall
On merit he confers, and freely all.
   Our list of nobles next let Amri grace,
Whose merits claimed the Abbethdin's high place;
Who with a loyalty that did excel
Brought all the endowments of Achitophel.
Sincere was Amri, and not only knew,
But Israel's sanctions into practice drew,
Our laws that did a boundless ocean seem
Were coasted all and fathomed all by him. 1020
No Rabbin speaks like him their mystic sense,
So just, and with such charms of eloquence,
To whom the double blessing does belong,
With Moses' inspiration Aaron's tongue.
   Than Sheva none more loyal zeal have shown,
Wakeful as Judah's lion for the crown,
Who for that cause still combats in his age
For which his youth with danger did engage.
In vain our factious priests the cant revive;
In vain seditious scribes with libel strive 1030
To inflame the crowd, while he with watchful eye
Observes, and shoots their treasons as they fly;
Their weekly frauds his keen replies detect,
He undeceives more fast than they infect.
So Moses, when the pest on legions preyed,
Advanced his signal, and the plague was stayed.
   Once more, my fainting Muse, thy pinions try,
And strength's exhausted store let love supply.
What tribute, Asaph, shall we render thee?
We'll crown thee with a wreath from thy own tree! 1040
Thy laurel grove no envy's flash can blast;

The song of Asaph shall for ever last!
With wonder late posterity shall dwell
On Absalom and false Achitophel:
Thy strains shall be our slumbering prophets' dream,
And, when our Sion virgins sing their theme,
Our jubilees shall with thy verse be graced;
The song of Asaph shall for ever last!
How fierce his satire loosed, restrained, how tame,
How tender of the offending young man's fame!   1050
How well his worth and brave adventures styled;
Just to his virtues, to his error mild.
No page of thine that fears the strictest view,
But teems with just reproof or praise as due;
Not Eden could a fairer prospect yield,
All Paradise without one barren field:
Whose wit the censure of his foes has past,
The song of Asaph shall for ever last!
What praise for such rich strains shall we allow?
What just rewards the grateful crown bestow?   1060
While bees in flowers rejoice, and flowers in dew,
While stars and fountains to their course are true,
While Judah's throne and Sion's rock stand fast,
The song of Asaph and the fame shall last.

Still Hebron's honoured happy soil retains
Our royal hero's beauteous dear remains:
Who now sails off, with winds nor wishes slack,
To bring his sufferings' bright companion back.
But ere such transport can our sense employ,
A bitter grief must poison half our joy;   1070
Nor can our coasts restored those blessings see
Without a bribe to envious destiny!
Curst Sodom's doom for ever fix the tide,
Where, by inglorious chance, the valiant died.
Give not insulting Askalon to know,
Nor let Gath's daughters triumph in our woe!

No sailor with the news swell Egypt's pride
By what inglorious fate our valiant died!
Weep, Arnon! Jordan, weep thy fountain's dry,
While Sion's rock dissolves for a supply. 1080
Calm were the elements, night's silence deep,
The waves scarce murmuring, and the winds asleep;
Yet fate for ruin takes so still an hour,
And treacherous sands the princely bark devour;
Then death unworthy seized a generous race,
To virtue's scandal and the stars' disgrace!
Oh! had the indulgent powers vouchsafed to yield,
Instead of faithless shelves, a listed field;
A listed field of Heaven's and David's foes,
Fierce as the troops that did his youth oppose, 1090
Each life had on his slaughtered heap retired,
Not tamely, and unconquering thus expired.
But Destiny is now their only foe,
And dying, even o'er that they triumph too;
With loud last breaths their master's scape applaud,
Of whom kind force could scarce the fates defraud:
Who for such followers lost (O matchless mind!)
At his own safety now almost repined!
Say, royal sir, by all your fame in arms,
Your praise in peace, and by Urania's charms, 1100
If all your sufferings past so nearly prest,
Or pierced with half so painful grief your breast?
Thus some diviner Muse her hero forms,
Not soothed with soft delights, but tost in storms,
Nor stretched on roses in the myrtle grove,
Nor crowns his days with mirth, his nights with love;
But far removed in thundering camps is found,
His slumbers short, his bed the herbless ground;
In tasks of danger always seen the first,
Feeds from the hedge and slakes with ice his thirst. 1110
Long must his patience strive with Fortune's rage,
And long opposing gods themselves engage;

E

Must see his country flame, his friends destroyed,
Before the promised empire be enjoyed :
Such toil of fate must build a man of fame,
And such to Israel's crown the godlike David came.

What sudden beams dispel the clouds so fast
Whose drenching rains laid all our vineyards waste?
The spring so far behind her course delayed
On the instant is in all her bloom arrayed ,   1120
The winds breathe low, the element serene,
Yet mark! what motion in the waves is seen
Thronging and busy as Hyblœan swarms
Or straggled soldiers summoned to their arms !
See where the princely bark in loosest pride,
With all her guardian fleet, adorns the tide !
High on her deck the royal lovers stand,
Our crimes to pardon ere they touched our land.
Welcome to Israel and to David's breast !
Here all your toils, here all your sufferings rest.   1130

This year did Ziloah rule Jerusalem.
And boldly all sedition's surges stem,
Howe'er encumbered with a viler pair
Than Ziph or Shimei, to assist the chair ;
Yet Ziloah's loyal labours so prevailed
That faction at the next election failed,
When even the common cry did justice sound,
And merit by the multitude was crowned :
With David then was Israel's peace restored,
Crowds mourned their error and obeyed their lord.   1140

KEY TO BOTH PARTS OF ABSALOM AND ACHITOPHEL.

(*From Vol. II. of* MISCELLANY POEMS, *Edition of* 1716.)

Abbethdin	Lord Chancellor.	*Ishban*	Sir R. Clayton.
Abdael .	Duke of Albemarle.	*Israel* .	England.
Absalom .	Duke of Monmouth.	*Issachar*	T. Thin, Esq.
Achitophel	Lord Shaftesbury.	*Jebusites*	Papists.
Adriel.	Earl of Musgrave.	*Jerusalem*	London.
Agag .	Sir E. B. Godfrey.	*Jonas* .	Sir W. Jones.
Amiel .	Mr. Seymour, Speaker.	*Jotham*	Marquis of Halifax.
Amri .	Lord Chancellor Finch.	*Jothran*	Lord Dartmouth.
Annabel	Duchess of Monmouth.	*Judas* .	Ferguson.
Arod .	Sir W. Waller.	*Mephibosheth*	Pordage.
Asaph .	Mr. Dryden.	*Michal*	Queen Katharine.
Balaam	Earl of Huntingdon.	*Nadab*	Lord Howard of Escrick.
Balak .	Burnet.	*Og* . .	Shadwell.
Barzillai .	Duke of Ormond.	*Othniel*	Duke of Grafton.
Bathsheba	Duchess of Portsmouth.	*Pharaoh*	French King.
Benaiah .	General Sackville.	*Phaleg*	Forbes.
Ben Jochanan	Johnson.	*Rabshakeh* .	Sir Thomas Player.
Bezaliel .	Duke of Beaufort.	*Sagan of Jeru-*}	}Bishop of London.
Caleb .	Lord Grey.	*salem,*	
Corah . . .	Dr. Oates.	*Sanhedrim* .	Parliament.
David .	King Charles II.	*Saul* . .	Oliver.
Doeg	Settle.	*Sheva* . .	Sir R. L'Estrange.
Egypt	France.	*Shimei*. .	Sheriff Bethel.
Eliab	Earl of Arlington.	*Solymean Rout*	London Rebels.
Ethnic Plot .	Popish Plot.	*Tyre* . . .	Holland.
Hebrew Priests{	{Church of England	*Uzza* . . .	J. H.
	Ministers.	*Western Dome*	Dolben.
Hebron . .	Scotland.	*Zadoch*	Archbishop Sancroft.
Helon . .	Lord Feversham.	*Zaken* .	Parliament-man.
Hushai	Earl of Rochester, Hyde.	*Ziloah* .	Sir J. Moor.
Isbosheth .	Richard Cromwell.	*Zimri*	Duke of Buckingham.

THE MEDAL.

A SATIRE AGAINST SEDITION.

"Per Graium populos mediæque per Elidis urbem
Ibat ovans, Divumque sibi poscebat honorem."
Virg. Æn. vi. 558.

EPISTLE TO THE WHIGS.

FOR to whom can I dedicate this poem with so much justice as to you? 'Tis the representation of your own hero: 'tis the picture drawn at length, which you admire and prize so much in little. None of your ornaments are wanting; neither the landscape of the Tower, nor the rising Sun, nor the *Anno Domini* of your new sovereign's coronation. This must needs be a grateful undertaking to your whole party: especially to those who have not been so happy as to purchase the original. I hear the graver has made a good 10 market of it: all his kings are bought up already; or the value of the remainder so enhanced, that many a poor Polander who would be glad to worship the image is not able to go to the cost of him, but must be content to see him here. I must confess I am no great artist; but sign-post painting will serve the turn to remember a friend by, especially when better is not to be had. Yet for your comfort the lineaments are true; and though he sate not five times to me, as he did to B., yet I have consulted history, as the Italian painters do, when they would draw a Nero or a

Caligula ; though they have not seen the man, they can help their imagination by a statue of him, and find out the colouring from Suetonius and Tacitus. Truth is, you might have spared one side of your Medal : the head would be seen to more advantage if it were placed on a spike of the Tower, a little nearer to the sun, which would then break out to better purpose. [You tell us in your Preface to the " No-Protestant Plot," that you shall be forced hereafter to leave off your modesty : I suppose you mean that little which is left you ; for it was worn to rags when you put out this Medal. Never 10 was there practised such a piece of notorious impudence in the face of an established government] I believe, when he is dead, you will wear him in thumb-rings, as the Turks did Scanderbeg, as if there were virtue in his bones to preserve you against monarchy. Yet all this while you pretend not only zeal for the public good, but a due veneration for the person of the King. But all men who can see an inch before them may easily detect those gross fallacies. That it is necessary for men in your circumstances to pretend both, is granted you ; for without them there could be no ground to 20 raise a faction. But I would ask you one civil question : What right has any man among you, or any association of men (to come nearer to you) who out of parliament cannot be considered in a public capacity, to meet, as you daily do, in factious clubs, to vilify the government in your discourses and to libel it in all your writings ? Who made you judges in Israel ? Or how is it consistent with your zeal of the public welfare to promote sedition ? Does your definition of loyal, which is to serve the King according to the laws, allow you the licence of traducing the executive power with which 30 you own he is invested ? You complain that his Majesty has lost the love and confidence of his people ; and by your very urging it you endeavour what in you lies to make him lose them. [All good subjects abhor the thought of arbitrary power, whether it be in one or many : if you were the patriots you would seem, you would not at this rate incense

the multitude to assume it ; for no sober man can fear it,
either from the King's disposition or his practice, or, even
where you would odiously lay it, from his Ministers.   Give us
leave to enjoy the government and the benefit of laws under
which we were born, and which we desire to transmit to our
posterity.   You are not the trustees of the public liberty :
and if you have not right to petition in a crowd, much less
have you to intermeddle in the management of affairs, or to
arraign what you do not like, which in effect is everything
10 that is done by the King and Council   Can you imagine
that any reasonable man will believe you respect the person
of his Majesty, when 'tis apparent that your seditious
pamphlets are stuffed with particular reflections on him ?
If you have the confidence to deny this, 'tis easy to be
evinced from a thousand passages, which I only forbear to
quote, because I desire they should die and be forgotten.   I
have perused many of your papers : and to show you that I
have, the third part of your "No-Protestant Plot" is, much
of it, stolen from your dead author's pamphlet, called the
20 "Growth of Popery," as manifestly as Milton's "Defence of
the English People" is from Buchanan, "De Jure Regni
apud Scotos," or your First Covenant and New Association
from the Holy League of the French Guisards.   Any one
who reads Davila may trace your practices all along.   There
were the same pretences for reformation and loyalty, the
same aspersions of the King, and the same grounds of a
rebellion.   I know not whether you will take the historian's
word, who says it was reported that Poltrot, a Hugonot,
murdered Francis, duke of Guise, by the instigations of
30 Theodore Beza, or that it was a Hugonot minister, otherwise called a Presbyterian (for our Church abhors so devilish
a tenet), who first writ a treatise of the lawfulness of de-
posing and murdering kings of a different persuasion in
religion : but I am able to prove from the doctrine of Calvin
and the principles of Buchanan, that they set the people
above the magistrate ; which, if I mistake not, is your own

fundamental, and which carries your loyalty no farther than your liking.] When a vote of the House of Commons goes on your side, you are as ready to observe it as if it were passed into a law; but when you are pinched with any former and yet unrepealed act of parliament, you declare that, in same cases, you will not be obliged by it. The passage is in the same third part of the "No-Protestant Plot," and is too plain to be denied. The late copy of your intended association you neither wholly justify nor condemn; but as the Papists, when they are unopposed, fly out into all 10 [the pageantries of worship, but in times of war, when they are hard pressed by arguments, lie close entrenched behind the Council of Trent, so now, when your affairs are in a low condition, you dare not pretend that to be a legal combination, but whensoever you are afloat, I doubt not but it will be maintained and justified to purpose.] For, indeed, there is nothing to defend it but the sword. 'Tis the proper time to say anything, when men have all things in their power.

In the mean time, you would fain be nibbling at a parallel betwixt this association and that in the time of Queen Eliza- 20 beth. But there is this small difference betwixt them, that the ends of the one are directly opposite to the other: one with the Queen's approbation and conjunction, as head of it; the other, without either the consent or knowledge of the King, against whose authority it is manifestly designed. Therefore, you do well to have recourse to your last evasion, that it was contrived by your enemies, and shuffled into the papers that were seized; [which yet you see the nation is not so easy to believe as your own jury. But the matter is not difficult, to find twelve men in Newgate who would acquit a 30 malefactor] = Shafto

I have one only favour to desire of you at parting, that when you think of answering this poem, you would employ the same pens against it who have combated with so much success against "Absalom and Achitophel;" for then you may assure yourselves of a clear victory, without the least

reply. Rail at me abundantly ; and, not to break a custom,
do it without wit. By this method you will gain a considerable point, which is wholly to wave the answer of my
arguments. Never own the bottom of your principles, for
fear they should be treason. Fall severely on the mis-
carriages of government : for, if scandal be not allowed, you
are no freeborn subjects. If God has not blessed you with
the talent of rhyming, make use of my poor stock and
welcome : let your verses run upon my feet ; and, for the
10 utmost refuge of notorious blockheads, reduced to the last
extremity of sense, turn my own lines upon me ; and, in
utter despair of your own satire, make me satirize myself.
Some of you have been driven to this bay already ; but,
above all the rest, commend me to the Nonconformist parson,
who writ the " Whip and Key." I am afraid it is not read
so much as the piece deserves, because the bookseller is every
week crying help at the end of his gazette, to get it off. You
see I am charitable enough to do him a kindness, that it may
be published as well as printed ; and that so much skill in
20 Hebrew derivations may not lie for waste-paper in the shop.
Yet I half suspect he went no farther for his learning, than
the index of Hebrew names and etymologies, which are
printed at the end of some English Bibles. If Achitophel
signify the brother of a fool, the author of that poem will
pass with his readers for the next of kin. And perhaps 'tis
the relation that makes the kindness. Whatever the verses
are, buy 'em up, I beseech you, out of pity ; for I hear the
conventicle is shut up, and the brother of Achitophel out of
service.

30 Now footmen, you know, have the generosity to make a
purse for a member of their society, who has had his livery
pulled over his ears ; and even Protestant socks are bought
up among you out of veneration to the name. A dissenter
in poetry from sense and English will make as good a Protestant rhymer, as a dissenter from the Church of England
a Protestant parson. Besides, if you encourage a young

beginner, who knows but he may elevate his style a little above the vulgar epithets of profane, and saucy Jack, and atheistic scribbler, with which he treats me, when the fit of enthusiasm is strong upon him; by which well-mannered and charitable expressions I was certain of his sect before I knew his name. What would you have more of a man? He has damned me in your cause from Genesis to the Revelations, and has half the texts of both the Testaments against me, if you will be so civil to yourselves as to take him for your interpreter, and not to take them for Irish witnesses. 10 After all, perhaps you will tell me, that you retained him only for the opening of your cause, and that your main lawyer is yet behind. Now if it so happen he meet with no more reply than his predecessors, you may either conclude that I trust to the goodness of my cause, or fear my adversary, or disdain him, or what you please, for the short on't is, 'tis indifferent to your humble servant, whatever your party says or thinks of him. 18

THE MEDAL.

A SATIRE AGAINST SEDITION.

OF all our antic sights and pageantry
Which English idiots run in crowds to see,
The Polish Medal bears the prize alone ;
A monster, more the favourite of the town
Than either fairs or theatres have shown.
Never did art so well with nature strive,
Nor ever idol seemed so much alive ;
So like the man, so golden to the sight,
So base within, so counterfeit and light.
One side is filled with title and with face ;   10
And, lest the king should want a regal place,
On the reverse a tower the town surveys,
O'er which our mounting sun his beams displays.
The word, pronounced aloud by shrieval voice,
Lætamur, which in Polish is *Rejoice,*
The day, month, year, to the great act are joined,
And a new canting holiday designed.
Five days he sate for every cast and look,
Four more than God to finish Adam took.
But who can tell what essence angels are   20
Or how long Heaven was making Lucifer ?
Oh, could the style that copied every grace
And ploughed such furrows for an eunuch face,

Could it have formed his ever-changing will,
The various piece had tired the graver's skill
A martial hero first, with early care
Blown, like a pigmy by the winds, to war ;
A beardless chief, a rebel ere a man,
So young his hatred to his Prince began.
Next this, (how wildly will ambition steer !)   30
A vermin wriggling in the usurper's ear,
Bartering his venal wit for sums of gold,
He cast himself into the saint-like mould ;
Groaned, sighed, and prayed, while godliness was gain,
The loudest bag-pipe of the squeaking train.
But, as 'tis hard to cheat a juggler's eyes,
His open lewdness he could ne'er disguise.
There split the saint ; for hypocritic zeal
Allows no sins but those it can conceal.
Whoring to scandal gives too large a scope ;   40
Saints must not trade, but they may interlope.
The ungodly principle was all the same ;
But a gross cheat betrays his partner's game.
Besides, their pace was formal, grave, and slack ;
His nimble wit outran the heavy pack.
Yet still he found his fortune at a stay,
Whole droves of blockheads choking up his way ;
They took, but not rewarded, his advice ;
Villain and wit exact a double price.
Power was his aim ; but thrown from that pretence, 50
The wretch turned loyal in his own defence,
And malice reconciled him to his Prince.
Him in the anguish of his soul he served,
Rewarded faster still than he deserved.
Behold him now exalted into trust,
His counsels oft convenient, seldom just ;
Even in the most sincere advice he gave
He had a grudging still to be a knave.
The frauds he learnt in his fanatic years

Made him uneasy in his lawful gears.   60
At best, as little honest as he could,
And, like white witches, mischievously good.
To his first bias longingly he leans
And rather would be great by wicked means.
Thus framed for ill, he loosed our triple hold,
(Advice unsafe, precipitous, and bold.)
From hence those tears, that Ilium of our woe ·
Who helps a powerful friend forearms a foe.
What wonder if the waves prevail so far,
When he cut down the banks that made the bar ?   70
Seas follow but their nature to invade ;
But he by art our native strength betrayed.
So Samson to his foe his force confest,
And to be shorn lay slumbering on her breast.
But when this fatal counsel, found too late,
Exposed its author to the public hate,
When his just sovereign by no impious way
Could be seduced to arbitrary sway,
Forsaken of that hope, he shifts his sail,
Drives down the current with a popular gale,   80
And shows the fiend confessed without a veil.
He preaches to the crowd that power is lent,
But not conveyed to kingly government,
That claims successive bear no binding force,
That coronation oaths are things of course ;
Maintains the multitude can never err,
And sets the people in the papal chair.
The reason's obvious, *interest never lies;*
The most have still their interest in their eyes,
The power is always theirs, and power is ever wise.   90
Almighty crowd ! thou shortenest all dispute.
Power is thy essence, wit thy attribute !
Nor faith nor reason make thee at a stay,
Thou leapst o'er all eternal truths in thy Pindaric way !
Athens, no doubt, did righteously decide,

When Phocion and when Socrates were tried ;
As righteously they did those dooms repent ;
Still they were wise, whatever way they went.
Crowds err not, though to both extremes they run ;
To kill the father and recall the son.   100
Some think the fools were most, as times went then,
But now the world's o'erstocked with prudent men.
The common cry is even religion's test ;
The Turk's is at Constantinople best,
Idols in India, Popery at Rome,
And our own worship only true at home,
And true but for the time ; 'tis hard to know
How long we please it shall continue so ;
This side to-day, and that to-morrow burns ;
So all are God Almighties in their turns.   110
A tempting doctrine, plausible and new ;
What fools our fathers were, if this be true !
Who, to destroy the seeds of civil war,
Inherent right in monarchs did declare ;
And, that a lawful power might never cease,
Secured succession to secure our peace.
Thus property and sovereign sway at last
In equal balances were justly cast ;
But this new Jehu spurs the hot-mouthed horse,
Instructs the beast to know his native force,   120
To take the bit between his teeth and fly
To the next headlong steep of anarchy.
Too happy England, if our good we knew,
Would we possess the freedom we pursue !
The lavish government can give no more ;
Yet we repine, and plenty makes us poor.
God tried us once ; our rebel fathers fought ;
He glutted them with all the power they sought,
Till, mastered by their own usurping brave,
The free-born subject sunk into a slave.   130
We loathe our manna, and we long for quails ;

Ah ! what is man, when his own wish prevails '
How rash, how swift to plunge himself in ill,
Proud of his power and boundless in his will !
That kings can do no wrong we must believe ;
None can they do, and must they all receive ?
Help, Heaven, or sadly we shall see an hour
When neither wrong nor right are in their power !
Already they have lost their best defence,
The benefit of laws which they dispense.   140
No justice to their righteous cause allowed,
But baffled by an arbitrary crowd ;
And medals graved, their conquest to record,
The stamp and coin of their adopted lord.

The man who laughed but once, to see an ass
Mumbling to make the cross-grained thistles pass,
Might laugh again to see a jury chaw
The prickles of unpalatable law.
The witnesses that, leech-like, lived on blood,
Sucking for them were med'cinally good ;   150
But when they fastened on their festered sore,
Then justice and religion they forswore,
Thus men are raised by factions and decried,
And rogue and saint distinguished by their side ;
They rack even Scripture to confess their cause
And plead a call to preach in spite of laws.
But that's no news to the poor injured page,
It has been used as ill in every age,
And is constrained with patience all to take,
For what defence can Greek and Hebrew make ?   160
Happy who can this talking trumpet seize,
They make it speak whatever sense they please '
'Twas framed at first our oracle to inquire ;
But since our sects in prophecy grow higher,
The text inspires not them, but they the text inspire.

London, thou great emporium of our isle,
O thou too bounteous, thou too fruitful Nile !
How shall I praise or curse to thy desert,
Or separate thy sound from thy corrupted part ?
I called thee Nile ; the parallel will stand :   170
Thy tides of wealth o'erflow the fattened land ;
Yet monsters from thy large increase we find
Engendered on the slime thou leavest behind.
Sedition has not wholly seized on thee,
Thy nobler parts are from infection free.
Of Israel's tribes thou hast a numerous band,
But still the Canaanite is in the land.
Thy military chiefs are brave and true,
Nor are thy disenchanted burghers few.
The head is loyal which thy heart commands,   180
But what's a head with two such gouty hands ?
The wise and wealthy love the surest way
And are content to thrive and to obey.
But wisdom is to sloth too great a slave ;
None are so busy as the fool and knave.
Those let me curse ; what vengeance will they urge,
Whose ordures neither plague nor fire can purge,
Nor sharp experience can to duty bring
Nor angry Heaven nor a forgiving king '
In gospel-phrase their chapmen they betray ;   190
Their shops are dens, the buyer is their prey ;
The knack of trades is living on the spoil ;
They boast e'en when each other they beguile.
Customs to steal is such a trivial thing
That 'tis their charter to defraud their King.
All hands unite of every jarring sect ;
They cheat the country first, and then infect.
They for God's cause their monarchs dare dethrone,
And they'll be sure to make His cause their own.
Whether the plotting Jesuit laid the plan   200
Of murdering kings, or the French Puritan,

Our sacrilegious sects their guides outgo
And kings and kingly power would murder too.

What means their traitorous combination less,
Too plain to evade, too shameful to confess?
But treason is not owned, when 'tis descried;
Successful crimes alone are justified.
The men who no conspiracy would find,
Who doubts but, had it taken, they had joined?
Joined in a mutual covenant of defence,   210
At first without, at last against their Prince?
If sovereign right by sovereign power they scan,
The same bold maxim holds in God and man
God were not safe; his thunder could they shun,
He should be forced to crown another son.
Thus, when the heir was from the vineyard thrown,
The rich possession was the murderers' own.
In vain to sophistry they have recourse;
By proving theirs no plot they prove 'tis worse,
Unmasked rebellion, and audacious force,   220
Which, though not actual, yet all eyes may see
'Tis working, in the immediate power to be;
For from pretended grievances they rise
First to dislike, and after to despise;
Then, Cyclop-like, in human flesh to deal,
Chop up a minister at every meal;
Perhaps not wholly to melt down the king,
But clip his regal rights within the ring;
From thence to assume the power of peace and war
And ease him by degrees of public care.   230
Yet, to consult his dignity and fame,
He should have leave to exercise the name,
And hold the cards while Commons played the game.
For what can power give more than food and drink,
To live at ease and not be bound to think?
These are the cooler methods of their crime,

But their hot zealots think 'tis loss of time ;
On utmost bounds of loyalty they stand,
And grin and whet like a Croatian band
That waits impatient for the last command :   240
Thus outlaws open villainy maintain ;
They steal not, but in squadrons scour the plain ;
And if their power the passengers subdue,
The most have right, the wrong is in the few.
Such impious axioms foolishly they show,
For in some soils Republics will not grow :
Our temperate Isle will no extremes sustain
Of popular sway or arbitrary reign :
But slides between them both into the best,
Secure in freedom, in a monarch blest.   250
And, though the climate, vexed with various winds,
Works through our yielding bodies on our minds,
The wholesome tempest purges what it breeds
To recommend the calmness that succeeds.

But thou, the pander of the people's hearts,
(O crooked soul and serpentine in arts !) . . .
What curses on thy blasted name will fall,
Which age to age their legacy shall call,   260
For all must curse the woes that must descend on all !
Religion thou hast none : thy mercury
Has passed through every sect, or theirs through thee.
But what thou givest, that venom still remains,
And the poxed nation feels thee in their brains.
What else inspires the tongues and swells the breasts
Of all thy bellowing renegado priests,
That preach up thee for God, dispense thy laws,
And with thy stum ferment their fainting cause,
Fresh fumes of madness raise, and toil and sweat,   270
To make the formidable cripple great ?

F

Yet should thy crimes succeed, should lawless power
Compass those ends thy greedy hopes devour,
Thy canting friends thy mortal foes would be,
Thy god and theirs will never long agree ;
For thine, if thou hast any, must be one
That lets the world and human kind alone ;
A jolly god that passes hours too well
To promise Heaven or threaten us with Hell,
That unconcerned can at rebellion sit   280
And wink at crimes he did himself commit.
A tyrant theirs ; the heaven their priesthood paints
A conventicle of gloomy sullen saints ;
A heaven, like Bedlam, slovenly and sad,
Foredoomed for souls with false religion mad.
    Without a vision poets can foreshow
What all but fools by common sense may know :
If true succession from our Isle should fail,
And crowds profane with impious arms prevail,
Not thou nor those thy factious arts engage   290
Shall reap that harvest of rebellious rage,
With which thou flatterest thy decrepit age.
The swelling poison of the several sects,
Which, wanting vent, the nation's health infects,
Shall burst its bag ; and fighting out their way,
The various venoms on each other prey.
The Presbyter, puffed up with spiritual pride,
Shall on the necks of the lewd nobles ride,
His brethren damn, the civil power defy,
And parcel out republic prelacy.   300
But short shall be his reign ; his rigid yoke
And tyrant power will puny sects provoke,
And frogs, and toads, and all the tadpole train
Will croak to Heaven for help from this devouring crane.
The cut-throat sword and clamorous gown shall jar
In sharing their ill-gotten spoils of war ;
Chiefs shall be grudged the part which they pretend ;

Lords envy lords, and friends with every friend
About their impious merit shall contend.
The surly Commons shall respect deny 310
And justle peerage out with property.
Their General either shall his trust betray
And force the crowd to arbitrary sway,
Or they, suspecting his ambitious aim,
In hate of kings shall cast anew the frame,
And thrust out Collatine that bore their name.

Thus inborn broils the factions would engage,
Or wars of exiled heirs, or foreign rage,
Till halting vengeance overtook our age,
And our wild labours, wearied into rest, 320
Reclined us on a rightful monarch's breast.

" *Pudet hæc opprobria vobis*
Et dici potuisse et non potuisse refelli."

MAC FLECKNOE;

OR,

A SATIRE ON THE TRUE BLUE PROTESTANT POET,

T. S.

MAC FLECKNOE.

ALL human things are subject to decay
And, when Fate summons, monarchs must obey.
This Flecknoe found, who, like Augustus, young
Was called to empire and had governed long,
In prose and verse was owned without dispute
Through all the realms of Nonsense absolute.
This aged prince, now flourishing in peace
And blest with issue of a large increase,
Worn out with business, did at length debate
To settle the succession of the state ;   10
And pondering which of all his sons was fit
To reign and wage immortal war with wit,
Cried, " 'Tis resolved, for Nature pleads that he
" Should only rule who most resembles me.
" Shadwell alone my perfect image bears,
" Mature in dulness from his tender years ;
" Shadwell alone of all my sons is he
" Who stands confirmed in full stupidity.
" The rest to some faint meaning make pretence,

! " But Shadwell never deviates into sense.   20
" Some beams of wit on other souls may fall,
" Strike through and make a lucid interval ;
" But Shadwell's genuine night admits no ray,
" His rising fogs prevail upon the day.
" Besides, his goodly fabric fills the eye
" And seems designed for thoughtless majesty,
" Thoughtless as monarch oaks that shade the plain
" And, spread in solemn state, supinely reign.
" Heywood and Shirley were but types of thee,
" Thou last great prophet of tautology.   30
" Even I, a dunce of more renown than they,
" Was sent before but to prepare thy way,
" And coarsely clad in Norwich drugget came
" To teach the nations in thy greater name.
" My warbling lute, the lute I whilom strung,
" When to King John of Portugal I sung,
" Was but the prelude to that glorious day,
" When thou on silver Thames didst cut thy way,
" With well-timed oars before the royal barge,
" Swelled with the pride of thy celestial charge,   40
" And, big with hymn, commander of an host ;
" The like was ne'er in Epsom blankets tost.
" Methinks I see the new Arion sail,
" The lute still trembling underneath thy nail.
" At thy well-sharpened thumb from shore to shore
" The treble squeaks for fear, the basses roar ;
" Echoes.from Pissing-alley Shadwell call,
" And Shadwell they resound from Aston-hall.
" About thy boat the little fishes throng,
" As at the morning toast that floats along.   50
" Sometimes, as prince of thy harmonious band,
" Thou wieldst thy papers in thy threshing hand.
" St. André's feet ne'er kept more equal time,
" Not even the feet of thy own ' Psyche's ' rhyme :
" Though they in number as in sense excel,

" So just, so like tautology, they fell
" That, pale with envy, Singleton forswore
" The lute and sword which he in triumph bore,
" And vowed he ne'er would act Villerius more."
Here stopped the good old sire and wept for joy,   60
In silent raptures of the hopeful boy.
All arguments, but most his plays, persuade
That for anointed dulness he was made.
   Close to the walls which fair Augusta bind,
(The fair Augusta much to fears inclined,)
An ancient fabric raised to inform the sight
There stood of yore, and Barbican it hight ;
A watch-tower once, but now, so fate ordains,
Of all the pile an empty name remains.
Near this a Nursery erects its head,   70
Where queens are formed and future heroes bred,
Where unfledged actors learn to laugh and cry,
Where infant punks their tender voices try,
And little Maximins the gods defy.
Great Fletcher never treads in buskins here,
Nor greater Jonson dares in socks appear ;
But gentle Simkin just reception finds
Amidst this monument of vanished minds ;
Pure clinches the suburbian muse affords
And Panton waging harmless war with words.   80
Here Flecknoe, as a place to fame well known,
Ambitiously designed his Shadwell's throne.
For ancient Decker prophesied long since
That in this pile should reign a mighty prince,
Born for a scourge of wit and flail of sense,
To whom true dulness should some " Psyches " owe,
But worlds of " Misers " from his pen should flow ;
" Humourists " and Hypocrites it should produce,
Whole Raymond families and tribes of Bruce.
   Now empress Fame had published the renown   90
Of Shadwell's coronation through the town.

Roused by report of fame, the nations meet
From near Bunhill and distant Watling-street.
No Persian carpets spread the imperial way,
But scattered limbs of mangled poets lay ;
Much Heywood, Shirley, Ogleby there lay,
But loads of Shadwell almost choked the way.
Bilked stationers for yoemen stood prepared
And Herringman was captain of the guard.
The hoary prince in majesty appeared,   100
High on a throne of his own labours reared.
At his right hand our young Ascanius sat,
Rome's other hope and pillar of the state.
His brows thick fogs instead of glories grace,
And lambent dulness played around his face.
As Hannibal did to the altars come,
Sworn by his sire a mortal foe to Rome ;
So Shadwell swore, nor should his vow be vain,
That he till death true dulness would maintain ;
And, in his father's right and realm's defence,   110
Ne'er to have peace with wit nor truce with sense.
The king himself the sacred unction made,
As king by office and as priest by trade.
In his sinister hand, instead of ball,
He placed a mighty mug of potent ale ·
"Love's Kingdom" to his right he did convey,
At once his sceptre and his rule of sway ;
Whose righteous lore the prince had practised young
And from whose loins recorded "Psyche" sprung.
His temples, last, with poppies were o'erspread,   120
That nodding seemed to consecrate his head.
Just at that point of time, if fame not lie,
On his left hand twelve reverend owls did fly.
So Romulus, 'tis sung, by Tiber's brook,
Presage of sway from twice six vultures took.
The admiring throng loud acclamations make
And omens of his future empire take.

The sire then shook the honours of his head,
And from his brows damps of oblivion shed
Full on the filial dulness : long he stood,   130
Repelling from his breast the raging God ;
At length burst out in this prophetic mood :
    " Heavens bless my son ! from Ireland let him reign
" To far Barbadoes on the western main ;
" Of his dominion may no end be known
" And greater than his father's be his throne ;
" Beyond 'Love's Kingdom' let him stretch his pen !"
He paused, and all the people cried "Amen."
Then thus continued he : "My son, advance
" Still in new impudence, new ignorance.   140
" Success let others teach, learn thou from me
" Pangs without birth and fruitless industry.
" Let 'Virtuosos' in five years be writ,
" Yet not one thought accuse thy toil of wit.
" Let gentle George in triumph tread the stage,
" Make Dorimant betray, and Loveit rage ;
" Let Cully, Cockwood, Fopling, charm the pit,
" And in their folly show the writer's wit.
" Yet still thy fools shall stand in thy defence
" And justify their author's want of sense.   150
" Let them be all by thy own model made
" Of dulness and desire no foreign aid,
" That they to future ages may be known,
" Not copies drawn, but issue of thy own.
" Nay, let thy men of wit too be the same,
" All full of thee and differing but in name.
" But let no alien Sedley interpose
" To lard with wit thy hungry Epsom prose.
" And when false flowers of rhetoric thou wouldst cull,
" Trust nature, do not labour to be dull ;   160
" But write thy best and top ; and in each line
" Sir Formal's oratory will be thine.
" Sir Formal, though unsought, attends thy quill

" And does thy northern dedications fill.
" Nor let false friends seduce thy mind to fame
" By arrogating Jonson's hostile name ;
" Let father Flecknoe fire thy mind with praise
" And uncle Ogleby thy envy raise.
" Thou art my blood, where Jonson has no part :
" What share have we in nature or in art ?   170
" Where did his wit on learning fix a brand
" And rail at arts he did not understand ?
" Where made he love in Prince Nicander's vein
" Or swept the dust in Psyche's humble strain ?
" When did his Muse from Fletcher scenes purloin,
" As thou whole Etherege dost transfuse to thine ?
" But so transfused as oil on waters flow,
" His always floats above, thine sinks below
" This is thy province, this thy wondrous way,
" New humours to invent for each new play :   180
" This is that boasted bias of thy mind,
" By which one way to dulness 'tis inclined,
" Which makes thy writings lean on one side still,
" And, in all changes, that way bends thy will.
" Nor let thy mountain belly make pretence
" Of likeness ; thine's a tympany of sense.
" A tun of man in thy large bulk is writ,
" But sure thou art but a kilderkin of wit.
" Like mine, thy gentle numbers feebly creep ;
" Thy tragic Muse gives smiles, thy comic sleep.   190
" With whate'er gall thou setst thyself to write,
" Thy inoffensive satires never bite ;
" In thy felonious heart though venom lies,
" It does but touch thy Irish pen, and dies.
" Thy genius calls thee not to purchase fame
" In keen Iambics, but mild Anagram.
" Leave writing plays, and choose for thy command
" Some peaceful province in Acrostic land.
" There thou mayest wings display and altars raise,

" And torture one poor word ten thousand ways;　200
" Or, if thou wouldst thy different talents suit,
" Set thy own songs, and sing them to thy lute."
He said, but his last words were scarcely heard,
For Bruce and Longville had a trap prepared,
And down they sent the yet declaiming bard.
Sinking he left his drugget robe behind,
Borne upwards by a subterranean wind.
The mantle fell to the young prophet's part
With double portion of his father's art.

NOTES.

FIRST PART OF ABSALOM AND ACHITOPHEL.

Preface.

P. 1, l. 5. **Whig and Tory.** The nickname Whig was conferred
on the Petitioners (see Introduction) in 1679. Two explanations
of it are given, one by Roger North in his *Examen*, p. 321 :
" The Anti-Exclusionists called their opponents ' Birmingham
Protestants,' alluding to false groats counterfeited at that place :
this held a considerable time but the word was not fluent enough
for hasty repartee : and after diverse changes the lot fell upon
Whig which was very significative as well as ready, being
vernacular in Scotland (from whence it was borrowed) for
corrupt and sour whey.' But Burnet's explanation, now generally received as the correct one, is this : " The south-west
counties of Scotland have seldom corn enough to serve them
round the year, and the northern parts producing more than
they need those in the west come in the summer to buy at Leith
the stores that come from the north : and from a word *whiggam*
used in driving their horses all that drove were called the
Whiggamors, and shorter the *Whigs*." It had been employed, he
adds, as a political designation in Scotland from the rising under
Argyll in 1648, subsequent to which " all that opposed the Court
came in contempt to be called *Whigs*" (*History of His Own Time*,
vol. i. p. 43). Tories was the nickname conferred in the same
year on the Abhorrers, and was derived from the Tories or Popish
banditti and bog-trotters in Ireland, the point being that they
were savages, robbers, and papists, and that the Duke of York
favoured the Irish. It has been variously derived from the Irish
words *toiridhe, tor, toraigheoir*, a pursuer ; *toirighim*, I follow
closely ; and *toir*, a corruption of *tabhair*, 'give there,' the supposed demand of a robber.

l. 11. **an Anti-Bromingham,** an anti-Whig.   See preceding note for the term Birmingham, and cf. the lines quoted by Mr. Christie,

> " No mobile gay fop
> With Bromingham pretences."

P. 2, ll. 4, 5. **Rebating the satire.**   To rebate is to blunt the edge (Old French *rebatre*).   Now obsolete, but common in Elizabethan and seventeenth century writers.   Mr. Christie quotes *Palamon and Arcite*, book ii. 502, " The keener edge of battle rebate."

ll. 11, 2. **tax their crimes,** censure.   Properly to put a rate upon.   French *taxer*, to tax or rate.

l. 17. **so unconscionable,** devoid of conscience or reason, unreasonable.

l. 24. **the character of Absalom.**   In dealing with Monmouth Dryden was in a very difficult position.   He knew that the King was in his heart greatly attached to his ' favourite son,' and that a reconciliation might take place.   " David himself could not be more tender of the young man's life than I would be of his reputation" are his words in the Preface.   It will be seen that throughout the poem he carefully abstains from all harsh censure, or rather contrives to flatter him.   All the blame is thrown on Shaftesbury.   " Were I the inventor ... I should certainly conclude the piece with the reconcilement of Absalon to David.   And who knows but this may come to pass?"

P. 3, l. 14. **to hope with Origen.**   The eminent Father of the Church, Origines Adamantius, born *circa* A.D. 186, died A.D. 253 or 254.   The reference is to an erroneous deduction from Origen's well-known doctrine of the universal restoration of the guilty. Origen, however, expressly asserts that the devil alone will suffer eternal punishment.

l. 24. **chirurgeon,** the obsolete form of surgeon.   From the Greek χειρουργία, a working with the hands, but immediately from the French *chirurgie.*

l. 25. **Ense rescindendum.**   From Ovid, *Met.* i. 191.

----

7. **Israel's monarch** etc., David, and so by analogy Charles II. Cf. i. *Samuel,* xiii. 14, " The Lord sought him a man after his own heart."   Cf. too *Acts,* xiii. 20.   These opening verses, in explaining the trouble caused by the King's having no legitimate issue, somewhat profanely palliate his notorious profligacy.   The reference, of course, is to his numerous children by his numerous mistresses.

11. **Michal, of royal blood,** Saul's daughter and David's wife = Catharine of Braganza, married to Charles II. in May, 1662, but she had borne him no children.

13. **several mothers.** Lucy Walters, mother of Monmouth and a daughter afterwards married to a Mr. William Sarsfield ; the Duchess of Cleveland, mother of the Duke of Southampton, the Duke of Grafton, the Duke of Northumberland, the Countess of Sussex, the Countess of Litchfield, and a daughter who became a nun ; the Duchess of Portsmouth, mother of the Duke of Richmond ; Nell Gynn, mother of the Duke of St. Albans and of James Beauclerk ; Mary Davis, Lady Shannon, and Catharine Peg, by whom Charles became the father respectively of Lady Derwentwater, the Countess of Yarmouth, and the Earl of Plymouth.

18. **Absalon,** Duke of Monmouth ; so spelt *metri gratiâ*.

21. **conscious destiny,** *i.e.* conscious of his worth, which predestined him to greatness.

23. **Early in foreign fields.** Monmouth served two campaigns as a volunteer in Louis XIV.'s army against the Dutch in 1672 and in 1673, particularly distinguishing himself at the siege of Maestricht. In 1678 he was in command of the British troops in coalition with the Dutch against the French, and again acquitted himself with great distinction in August, 1678, at the battle of St. Denis.

24. **allied to Israel's crown,** Holland and France.

26. **as he were,** as if he were, a not uncommon ellipse. Cf. *Macbeth,* i. 4, "as 'twere a careless trifle."

29. **accompanied with grace.** In this, and above, we have allusions to Monmouth's great personal beauty. See Introduction.

30. **And Paradise,** etc. Pope echoes this line—
"And Paradise was open'd on the wild."
—*Eloisa to Abelard,* 133.

32. **His youthful image.** Cf. Livy, lib. xx. cap. 1, of the young Hannibal, "Hamilcarem juvenem redditum sibi veteres milites credere."

34. **the charming Annabel,** Monmouth's wife, Anne Scott, Countess of Buccleuch, the only surviving daughter of Francis, Earl of Buccleuch, and one of the richest heiresses in Europe. They were married in April, 1663. Her charms have been celebrated both by Madam Dunois and Evelyn. She was a patroness of Dryden, who dedicated *The Indian Emperor* to her.

39. **And Amnon's murder.** This allusion has never been satisfactorily explained. Sir Walter Scott supposes it to refer to the slitting of Sir John Coventry's nose by Monmouth's agency, in consequence of a sarcastic allusion of Coventry's in the House of Commons to the King's amours. But this was not murder.

Others explain it as a reference to a disgraceful affair of which
Andrew Marvel, in a letter dated Feb. 28th, 1671, gives an
account : " On Saturday night last, or rather Sunday morning at
two o'clock, some persons reported to be of great quality, together
with other gentlemen, set upon the watch, and killed a poor
beadle praying for his life upon his knees, with many wounds."
Adding in another letter : "Doubtless you have heard how
Monmouth, Albemarle, Dunbane, etc., fought with the watch
and killed a poor beadle : they have all got their pardon for Monmouth's sake, but it is an act of great scandal." See too *State
Poems*, vol. i. p. 147. But Dryden is hardly likely to have
designated a beadle as Amnon, and the affair had no connection
with "revenge for injur'd fame." It appears to be an allusion
to some other passage in Monmouth's life on which light has yet
to be thrown.

42. **in Sion**, London.

43. **sincerely blest**, purely, truly. The old derivation from
sine and *cerâ* is doubted by Skeat, who thinks it means wholly
separated, from *sin* and *cerus*, from *cernere*, to separate. Dryden
is fond of it in the Latin sense, the sense in which it is here used.
Cf. *Annus Mirabilis*, 209, " But ah, how *insincere* are all our
joys," and *Pal. and Arcite*, "And none can boast sincere felicity."

45. **The Jews**, the English.

51. **These Adam-wits**. Wits, who having all the freedom of
Adam, "for one restraint lord of the world besides," still chafed
against the slight restriction placed on them.

57. **Saul**, Oliver Cromwell.

58. **foolish Ishbosheth**, Richard Cromwell, who on the death
of his father succeeded to the Protectorship, which he was
practically forced into resigning when he dissolved Parliament in
April 22nd, 1659. " He was," says Mrs. Hutchinson (*Life of
Colonel Hutchinson*, p. 345, "a meeke, temperate, and quiett
man, but had not a spirit fit to succeed his father, or to manage
such a perplexed government."

59. **did from Hebron bring**. Hebron in the Second Part of
this poem means Scotland, and assuming that the same significa-
tion is given to it here, it may be a reference to Monk's march
from Scotland between December, 1659, and February, 1660,
which practically brought about the Restoration ; or it may be a
reference to the fact that Charles had been already crowned King
of Scotland. We should naturally expect it to mean the Nether-
lands or Brussels, where Charles was residing when he received
the invitation to return, as King, to England.

61. **Those very Jews**. The object of the following verses is to
cast discredit on the Whigs, whose share in the Restoration is

attributed not to an honourable and loyal desire to have their King back again, but to mere restlessness and whim.

72. **dishonest**, in the Latin sense of the term, cf. the use of the word *inhonestus*, ugly, unseemly. Dryden is fond of this use of it. Thus in the *Fables*, "Dishonest with lop'd arms the youth appears"; as in *Alexander's Feast*, he used honest for handsome—

> " Flush'd with a purple grace,
> He shows his *honest* face."

75. **thus qualified.** Having these qualities, this temper.

86. **Were Jebusites**, Roman Catholics. Dryden now proceeds to review the position of the Papists in England and the events which led to the Popish Plot.

87. **the native right.** This half-finished line is no doubt in imitation of Virgil's hemistichs. Cowley is guilty of the same affectation in his *Davideis*, and so also are Oldham in his *Satires on the Jesuits* and Young in his *Night Thoughts*.

88. **the chosen people**, the Protestants. The lines which follow with reference to their impoverishment and their being "deprived of all command," are allusions to the numerous statutes which had, since the accession of Elizabeth, been promulgated for the suppression of popery, and more particularly to the severe statutes which had been passed and enforced since the accession of Charles II. "Their gods disgraced and burnt like common wood," is an allusion not only to the wholesale destruction of images and relics at the Reformation, but to what regularly occurred on every anniversary of the 5th of November.

100. **Of whatsoe'er descent.** With this rough wit may be compared Horace, *Sat.* I. viii. 1-3.

104. **The Jewish Rabbins.** Doctors of the Church of England, the Protestant divines. This is what grammarians called a *nominativus pendens*, there is no verb. Dryden is often very lax in his syntax, cf. ll. 90-1 *supra*.

108. **that Plot**, the Popish Plot, originated in the autumn of 1678, by Titus Oates and his accomplices. See Introduction and cf. Lingard, *Hist. of England*, vol. ix. p. 346 *seqq.*

111. **With oaths affirmed, with dying oaths denied.** Affirmed on oath by Oates and Bedloe, denied with " dying oaths " by Coleman (*State Trials*, vii. 1. 78), by Ireland, Grove, and Pickering (*Id.* viii. 79. 143), and Hill, Green, and Berry (*Id.* vii. 159-230).

114. **some truth there was.** That there was some slight foundation for Oates's assertions is generally acknowledged by contemporary and subsequent historians.

114. **dashed.** To dash is to disturb by throwing in, so to mix or adulterate. The image is from a pot boiling.

118. **Egyptian rites,** French. Since the marriage of Charles I. with Henrietta Maria, France was, in the English mind, always associated with Roman Catholicism. These lines are a coarse sneer at the doctrine of transubstantiation which was afterwards to find so powerful and eloquent an apologist in Dryden.

121. **for worship and for good.** Borrowed from Juvenal, *Sat.* xi. 10, 1—

> " O sanctas gentes, quibus hæc nascuntur in hortis
> Numina."

128. **Hebrew priests,** the clergy of the Church of England. He had said above that " priests of all religions are the same," and this satire on the Protestant clergy is as severe as that against the Roman Catholics.

130. **meant to slay.** The reference is to the alleged project of Pickering, Groves, and Ireland to assassinate the King in April 1678. See Hargrave's *State Trials*, vol. ii. p. 754.

134. **for want of common** sense. Had it not been for the incredible recklessness of Oates and his accomplices there can be little doubt that the Whigs would have carried all before them.

140. **several factions.** Dryden here explains the relation of the Popish Plot to the projects of Shaftesbury and his accomplices, how they utilized the excitement which it had caused.

142. **Some by their friends.** The references in these lines appear to have special relation (*a*) to the Earl of Huntingdon and Lord Grey of Wark, (*b*) to the Duke of Buckingham (see particularly lines 563, 4), and (*c*) to Shaftesbury.

153. **bold.** The epithet may be applied with propriety to the general daring of Shaftesbury's designs, but cautious timidity was what, through life, most distinguished him personally.

158. **pigmy body.** Properly pygmy, cf. French pygmée, Greek, πυγμαῖος. The Pygmæi were a fabulous nation of dwarfs who are said to have lived in Æthiopia, and were no more than a span long, hence their name from πυγμη. Hence the name has come to be synonymous with dwarfs. References to Shaftesbury's puny figure are common in the satires and broadsides of the time.

163. **to madness near allied.** Cf. Seneca, *De Tranquillitate animi,* xv., " nullum magnum ingenium sine mixturâ dementiæ fuit."

170. **that unfeathered two-legged thing.** Plato's famous ζῷον, δίπουν ἄπτερον, an animal with two feet and unfledged, which he is said to have given as a definition of a man. The reference is to Anthony Ashley Cooper, second Earl of Shaftesbury, and

father of the author of the *Characteristics*, the philosopher and critic. The second Earl was not born " a shapeless lump "; he was a very handsome man, but stupid and foolish we are told.

175. **the triple bond he broke.** The Triple Alliance between England, Sweden, and Holland, arranged by Sir William Temple in Jan. 1667-8, was broken by the war declared against Holland in March 1672, and Shaftesbury had been one of the most active promoters of that war.

177. **a foreign yoke.** An allusion to the secret alliance of Charles II. with Louis XIV., in 1670, by the Treaty of Dover. Mr. Christie has shown that Shaftesbury was not privy to this, although he supported the war against Holland.

179. **Usurped a patriot's ... name.** This refers to Shaftesbury putting himself at the head of the Country Party and the Petitioners.

180. **So easy still it proves** etc. These lines were added in the second edition. There is an absurd story that Dryden introduced them to soften his attack on Shaftesbury, because the Earl had procured a nomination of one of Dryden's sons to the Charter-house. The fact is that Shaftesbury made a very good Lord Chancellor, a. fact which was notorious, and Sir Walter Scott well observes that these and other passages, in which Dryden has softened the severity of his satire, illustrate not only the poet's taste and judgment, but " that tone of honorable and just feeling which distinguishes a true satire from a libellous lampoon." Pope, see his character of Atticus in the *Prologue to the Satires*, and Churchill, in his *Epistle to Hogarth*, have shown that the judicious mixture of praise adds pungency to censure, ' as the soft plume gives swiftness to the dart.'

188. **an Abbethdin.** The Abbethdin was president of the Jewish judicature, literally father (*ab*) of the house of judgment (*bethdin*),—Christie.

195. **cockle,** a weed which grows in cornfields ; is supposed to choke and hinder the growth of the corn. " Let thistles grow instead of wheat, and cockle instead of barley " (*Job*, xxxi. 40).

196. **David for him.** David, all of whose Psalms are in honour of Heaven, would have composed a Psalm in his honour, and so Heaven would have been deprived of one Psalm at least.

198. **But wild ambition.** This couplet, as Macaulay has pointed out, is taken almost verbatim from a couplet placed under the frontispiece of Knolles' *History of the Turks*—

> " Greatnesse on goodnesse loves to slide, not stand,
> And leaves for Fortune's ice Virtue's firm land."

204. **manifest of crimes,** clearly convicted of, exactly the Latin phrase *manifestus sceleris*. Cf. Sallust, *Jugurth*. 39,

"Jugurtha manifestus tanti sceleris." Mr. Christie also com-
pares *Palamon and Arcite*, bk. i. 623—

" Calisto there stood manifest of shame."

205. He stood at bold defiance. What drove Shaftesbury into
opposition to the Court was that the King, alarmed at the
remonstrances of the people against popery, broke the seal he
had affixed to the Declaration of Indulgence, and so deceived his
ministers and exposed them to the fury of the Commons. "The
Cabal took the same sudden turn with the King, Shaftesbury
observing that 'the prince who forsook himself deserved to be
forsaken.' He then put himself at the head of the opposition to
the Court." (Dalrymple's *Memoirs*, vol. i. p. 35).

208. The wished occasion. Though Shaftesbury may perhaps
be absolved from the charge of complicity in the invention of the
Popish Plot, there can be no doubt that he utilized it.

213. And proves the King etc. We now know certainly, and
it was known to some even then, that Charles II. had p   l
declared himself a Roman Catholic in 1669, and had nhartly
afterwards made a secret engagement with Louis XIV. to
establish popery in England. So, as Mr. Christie observes,
Shaftesbury invented no calumny.

215. easy to rebel, easily disposed to rebellion. A Latin
idiom, 'callidus coudere,' 'celer excipere.' So in the Psalms,
" Their feet are *swift to shed blood*."

219. natural instinct. Note the accent is on the last syllable,
as it almost always is in the writers of the 17th century.

222. Not that he wished. Dryden represents Shaftesbury as
a pure demagogue, and these lines give us the key to his policy,
which, according to Dryden, was not really to exalt Monmouth,
but to restore a republic with himself as its dictator.

230. Auspicious prince. The whole of this passage to line 272 is
a noble illustration of Dryden's magnificent rhetoric, of that union
of sweetness with strength, of massiveness with flexibility, which
distinguishes his rhythm, of the vigour, incisiveness, and power of
his style. It is when reading passages like these that we can feel
the propriety of what Pope and Gray have written about him—

" Dryden taught to join
The varying verse, the full resounding line,
The long majestic march and energy divine."
Imitation of Horace, First Epistle of the Second Book.

See too Gray's *Bard*—

"Behold where Dryden's less presumptuous care,
Wide o'er the fields of glory bear
Two courses of ethereal race,
With necks in thunder cloth'd and long-resounding pace."

240. **Thee Saviour, thee.** Imitation of the Latin. Cf. Lucretius, i. 6, "Te, Dea, Te fugiunt venti." Milton has also imitated it, "Thee, Shepherd, thee, the woods etc. ... mourn" (*Lycidas*, 39).

242. **pomps.** In the Greek and Latin sense "processions."

251. **Or ... or.** A poetical construction, not allowable in prose.

252. **Heaven has to all** etc. An observation which has found expression in the celebrated passage in *Julius Cæsar*, Act iv. Sc. 3, "There is a tide in the affairs of men" etc. And cf. Chapman, *Bussy D'Ambois*, Act i. Sc. 1—

"There is a deep nick in time's restless wheel
For each man's good, when which nick comes, it strikes."

261. **spreads her locks.** An allusion to the ancient picture of Opportunity who has a fore-lock but is bald behind. "Fronte capillata est, post hæc occasio calva."

264. **At Gath,** Brussels.

270. **Jordan's sand,** the beach at Dover.

275. **one poor Plot,** the Popish Plot.

280. **Naked of friends.** A common construction in Greek and Latin, γύμνος φίλων, mors famæ nuda. Dryden is very fond of this construction. Cf. "turbulent of wit" (153), "swift of despatch" (191), "unblam'd of life" (479).

281. **Pharaoh,** Louis XIV., King of France (Egypt).

299. **And nobler is a limited** etc. "The legitimacy of the Duke of Monmouth, though boldly and repeatedly asserted by his immediate partizans, did not receive general credit even in the popular faction. It was one of Shaftesbury's advantages to have chosen for the ostensible head of his party a candidate whose right had he ever attained to the crown, must have fluctuated between an elective and hereditary title. The consciousness of how much he was to depend on Shaftesbury's arts obliged the Duke to remain at the devotion of that intriguing politician" (Scott's *Note*).

303. **What cannot praise** etc. Observe the skill with which all blame is diverted from Monmouth and thrown on Shaftesbury, and the art with which the Duke and his royal father are flattered.

305. **Desire of power.** Cf. Pope's lines in the *Elegy to the Memory of an Unfortunate Lady*—

"Ambition first sprang from your blest abodes,
The glorious fault of angels and of gods,
Thence to their images on earth it flows,
And in the breasts of kings and heroes glows.'

310. **angel's metal.** Properly a metal or mineral. Greek

μέταλλον, a mine; Latin *metallum*; then it comes to mean temper, then courage, spirit. It is generally spelt mettle.

336. **popularly mad.** Run mad after the people, or to please, gain the applause, of the people. Cf. Latin 'populariter.' Cf. Juvenal, *Sat.* iii. 37, "Quem libet occidunt populariter," and Dryden's version of the passage "With thumbs bent back they *popularly* kill"; and see also *infra*, 490, "And *popularly* prosecute the plot"; again *infra*, 689, "bowing *popularly* low."

344. **Prevents,** anticipates, out-runs.

346. **diadem,** ensign of royalty bound about the head of an Oriental monarch; from διά and δέω.

350. **And late augment.** Notice how the wish is infused in the statement. Cf. Hor. *Odes,* I. ii., "Serus in cælum redeas."

353. **His brother,** James, Duke of York. Dryden has drawn the same false character of James in the *Duke of Guise,* Act v. Sc. 1.

390. **Sanhedrin,** the Parliament. It was the highest council of the Jews.

401. **The** next **successor,** James, Duke of York; the arts referred to in the next line are Shaftesbury's intrigues for passing the Exclusion Bill.

411. **All empire.** Cf. Junius, *Letter* i., "The submission of a free people to the executive authority of government is no more than a compliance with laws which they themselves have enacted."

418. **God was their King.** The republic which acknowledged God alone for their king, but which was dispossessed by Cromwell (Saul). Cf. line 522, "their old beloved theocracy."

419. **piety.** In the Latin sense "affection for your father."

425. **fond,** foolish. It is the preterite of the A.S. verb *fonnen,* to act foolishly.

461. **Prevail yourself of what** etc. A French idiom borrowed from *se prevaloir de,* to take advantage of, to profit by. Cf. Preface to *Annus Mirabilis,* "Yet I could not *prevail myself* of it in the English." Dryden's diction is frequently deformed not only by Gallicisms of this kind, but by the employment of French words instead of their English equivalents. Cf. for a few examples among many *Astræa Redux,* 203; *Poem on the Coronation,* 120; *Hind and Panther,* Part i. 388, Part iii. 511, and Part ii. 648, 227. It is an interesting illustration of the influence exercised by the French language and literature on our own during the latter part of the seventeenth century. See Macaulay's remarks, *History,* vol. i. ch. 3. Johnson, in his Life of Dryden, has commented with just severity on these innovations.

480. **Not stained** etc. Note again the great tenderness with which Monmouth is treated.

492. **The malcontents.** Notice how admirably the various motives of Shaftesbury's different tools are described.

508. **husbandry,** *sc.* good management, thrift. From the Icelandic *húsbóndi*, the master or goodman of the house. Cf. Shakespeare, " There's *husbandry* in heaven," *Macbeth*, Act ii. Sc. 1.

513. **Solymæan rout,** the mob of London.

517. **Ethnic plot.** This means Protestant, or, following the analogy, a Gentile plot in opposition to a Jebusite or Papist.

519. **Hot Levites.** The Presbyterian ministers who had been displaced by the Act of Uniformity (Christie).

522. **theocracy.** See note on line 418.

525. **Aaron's race.** The clergy,—with another sneer at them.

544. **Zimri.** George Villiers, the second Duke of Buckingham, was the son of the favourite of Charles I. He was born 30th January, 1627, and, after a long career of profligacy and folly, he died at Kirby Moorside, 17th April, 1687. See Pope's brilliant and impressive picture of Buckingham's death and character, *Moral Essays*, Epist. iii. 299 *seqq.* He died at the house of one of his tenants and not at a poor inn as Pope has—*splendide mendax*—represented. His character has been elaborately delineated by Burnet, *Hist. of his Own Times*, vol. i. p. 100, by Count Hamilton in *Grammont's Memoirs*, by Butler, both in verse and prose, in his *Miscellaneous Works*, by Duke in his vigorous Drydenian poem the *Review*, and by Walpole in his *Royal and Noble Authors*,—all of which form admirable commentaries on Dryden's portrait. Dryden's model was undoubtedly Horace's portrait of Tigellius, *Sat.* I. iii. 1-20, with a touch or two from Juvenal's Greek parasite, *Sat.* iii. 73-7. Dryden was very proud of this character and thought it " worth the whole poem ": see his interesting remarks on it in his *Essay on Satire*.

563. **laughed himself from court.** A reference to Buckingham's foolish plot against the King in 1667, in consequence of which he was obliged to conceal himself ; but afterwards surrendering he was confined to the Tower, till the King, moved by the mingled threats and entreaties of the Duchess of Cleveland, set him free. See for a full account of all this Jesse's *Court of England under the Stuarts*, vol. iii. p. 83 *seqq.*

574. **well-hung Balaam,** the Earl of Huntingdon, one of the seventeen peers who signed the petition entreating the King to have recourse to the advice of his parliament ; he was also the one chosen to present it, 7th Dec., 1679. He was one of the petitioners to the King in 1681 against holding the Parliament

at Oxford, and was thoroughly obnoxious to the Court.   The explanation of the epithet in the text had better be left where it is
to be found in Luttrel's MSS. :   cold Caleb, Lord Grey of Wark,
who is said to have been so callous (hence the epithet) and des-
picable as to allow Monmouth to intrigue with his wife.   He was
subsequently engaged in the Rye House Plot, and landed with
Monmouth at Lyme in 1685 : he was present at the skirmish at
Bridport and at the Battle of Sedgemoor, in both of which en-
gagements he disgraced himself by his cowardice.   A criminal
intrigue with his sister-in-law led to a famous trial.   See Howell's
State Trials, ix. 127.   He subsequently became Earl of Tanker-
ville and in 1699 was First Lord of the Treasury.   For his
character see Macaulay, *Hist.* vol. iv. p. 314-5.

575, 6. canting **Nadab** ... **paschal lamb**, Lord Howard of
Escricke, one of the most amusing but abandoned men of the age,
and one of the most intimate associates of Monmouth and Shaftesbury.   Dryden's reference is to this : The informer Fitzharris
had written a shameful libel against the Court, was convicted of
high treason, and to save his life, which was however forfeited,
asserted that Lord Howard had instigated him to forge a docu-
ment incriminating the Queen and the Duke of York.   Howard
was accordingly sent to the Tower where he published a declaration asserting his innocence, and this he is said to have confirmed
by taking the sacrament in lamb's wool, *i.e.* ale poured on roasted
apples and sugar.   Mr. Christie quotes two passages from contemporary satires referring to this profanity—

" With Mahomet wine he damneth, with intent
    To erect his paschal lamb's wool sacrament."
                              Absalon's Nine Worthies.

He was afterwards involved in the Rye House Plot, and to save
his own life basely informed against Algernon Sidney, Russel,
and Hampden.   Dryden's expression is as coarse and profane as
the act which he reprobates.

581. **bull-faced Jonas**, Sir William Jones, a very able, and, it
is said, honest lawyer.   He became Serjeant-at-Law in 1669,
Solicitor-General in Nov. 1673, Attorney-General in June, 1675,
and he died in 1682.   "He was," says Burnet, *Own Times*, "no
flatterer, but a man of morose temper, so he was against all
the measures that they took at Court."   See North's *Examen*,
507-10, and cf. the virulent epitaph on Jones in the *State
Poems*, vol. iii. p. 157.   As Attorney-General he had conducted
the prosecutions against those engaged in the Popish Plot ; but
some time after he resigned office and joined the Opposition.   He
drew up the Habeas Corpus Act, and probably, Mr. Christie
thinks, the Exclusion Bill.

585. **Shimei, whose youth** etc., Slingsby Bethel, son of Sir

Walter Bethel, a staunch Royalist, who was beheaded by Crom-well's High Court of Justice. But the son did not follow in the father's footsteps, being a notorious republican. A very cele-brated pamphlet, *The World's Mistake in Oliver Cromwell*, was ascribed to him. In 1680 he was chosen one of the sheriffs of the City of London, and to qualify himself for his office renounced the Covenant, received the Sacrament, but adhered to his factious principles. Eccentric and mean, he kept no table, but lived at a chop-house, giving no entertainment during the whole of his shrievalty. "He turned," says Burnet, "from the ordinary way of a sheriff's living into the extreme of sordidness" (*Own Time*, l. 480). His stinginess passed into a proverb, and 'to Bethel the city' became a phrase used to describe a sheriff who gave poor entertainments.

595. **a vare**, a wand ; from the Spanish *vara*. Mr. Christie appositely quotes Howel's *Familiar Letters* (p. 161, ed. 1728), "The proudest don of Spain when he is prancing upon his genet ... if an alguazil show him his *vare*, that is a little white staff he carrieth as a badge of his office," etc.

614, 5. **by writing ... That kings were useless**, an allusion to a tract lately published anonymously by Bethel, entitled *Interests of Princes and States*.

617. **Rechabite.** The Rechabites were the tribe or family of Kenites whom Jonadab, the son of Rechab, subjected to a new rule of life. One of their characteristics was total abstinence from wine ; see *Jeremiah*, xxxv. 1-6, "Jonadab the son of Rechab our father commanded us, saying, Ye shall drink no wine, neither ye nor your sons for ever."

632. **Corah**, Titus Oates, the son of an Anabaptist ribbon-weaver (l. 639). He is said to have been educated at Merchant Tailors' School, and to have gone from thence to Cambridge. He then took orders, and officiated as a curate in Kent and Sussex, but, being guilty of gross immorality, he was suspended. He then went over to the Church of Rome, and obtained admission into the Jesuits' College at St. Omer. Returning to England, he concocted the infamous fictions about the alleged conspirators in the Popish Plot. For the supposed service he had thus done the King he received a pension of £1200, was lodged in White-hall, and protected by guards. On the accession of James II. pro-ceedings were taken against him, and an enormous fine imposed ; finally he was tried for perjury. After changing his religion several times, he died nominally a Baptist in 1705.

646. **Sunk were his** eyes. North gives a full description of Oates (*Examen*, p. 225). See, too, Macaulay, *Hist.* i. p. 227.

649. **A church vermilion**, the ruddy complexion of a parson-

Trulliber, facetiously compared to the shining face of Moses when coming from the mount (*Exodus*, xxxiv. 29-35), proved his sanctity.

658. **Rabbinical degree,** Oates asserted that he had received the degree of Doctor of Divinity from the University of Salamanca. Cf. Dryden's Epilogue to *Mithridates*—

"Our colleges give no degrees for hire,
    Would Salamanca were a little nigher."

676. **for Agag's murder call.** Sir Edmund Bury Godfrey was the magistrate before whom Oates had affirmed on oath his account of the Popish Plot. Not long afterwards, Sir Edmund was found in a ditch on Primrose Hill murdered, with his own sword thrust through his body. As Sir Edmund had been unwilling to receive the depositions of Oates, and was reputed to be friendly to the Papists, Dryden implies that he was murdered, as a friend of the Roman Catholics, at the instigation of Oates.

677. **In terms as coarse.** See the *First Book of Samuel*, ch. xv., where the prophet rebukes Saul for sparing Agag.

680. **predicament,** a logical term originally meaning the state, situation, or condition on which certain affirmations may be made or certain inferences drawn.

691. **repeats their names,** this weakness in human nature was so flattered by the Romans that a nomenclator always followed at the side of the popularity-hunting grandee. "Gaudent prænomine molles Auriculæ" (Hor. *Sat.* II. v. 32, 3).

697. **than Hybla drops.** Mount Hybla in Sicily was famous for its bees and honey. Cf. Homer, *Il.* i. 249, τοῦ καὶ ἀπὸ γλώσσης μέλιτος γλυκίων ῥέεν αὐδή.

700. **a banished man,** "Monmouth had been sent out of England by the King in September, 1679; he returned without permission in November. The King then ordered him to quit England, and he disobeyed. He was then deprived of all his offices, and banished from Court" (Christie).

705. **Egypt and Tyrus,** France and Holland.

710. **Bathsheba,** the Duchess of Portsmouth, Louise de Querouaille. She appeared first in the train of the Duchess of Orleans in 1670, when she fascinated Charles; she was created Duchess of Portsmouth in 1673, and was now (1681) the reigning Sultana.

727. **The crowd.** These lines describe the progress which, at the advice of Shaftesbury, Monmouth made in 1680 through Lancashire, Staffordshire, Worcestershire, Cheshire, Devonshire, and Somerset. For a graphic corroboration of Dryden's picture, see Dalrymple's *Memoirs*, vol. i. p. 55.

738. **Wise Issacar**, Thomas Thynne of Langleat, one of the richest Commoners in England, and called from his great wealth 'Tom of Ten Thousand.' He had formerly been a friend and favourite of the Duke of York, but afterwards quarrelling with him, he joined Monmouth's party, and entertained him most magnificently on the occasion of the progress mentioned. He was afterwards (Feb., 1682) murdered by assassins employed by Count Koningsmark.

750. **by a brother and a wife.** What had enabled Shaftesbury and his partizans to foment their plots and so endanger the King's life was (a) that the King's brother, the Duke of York, was a Papist, and (b) that the Queen having no children the succession to the throne was in dispute.

753. **O foolish Israel.** The lines which follow are a striking illustration of one of Dryden's distinguishing characteristics, his power of reasoning vigorously and cogently in verse.

785. **What standard is** there etc. This very obscure couplet appears to mean : What standard or test has an unstable and disorderly multitude, which, if it has for a moment a common aim, wastes and exhausts itself all the faster. The metaphor is from water which in flowing to a mark, and so acquiring impetus, is by its very impetus carried on and past—into waste.

804. **to touch our ark.** Here metaphorically used for what is most sacred among the Israelites, as it was forbidden on pain of death for any save the priests to touch the ark.

816. **Some let me name.** Dryden now passes in review the statesmen who were loyal to Charles and the Court party. The Duke of Ormond (Barzillai), Sancroft, Archbishop of Canterbury (Zadoc), Compton, Bishop of London (the Sagan of Jerusalem), Dolben, Bishop of Rochester (Him of the western dome), the Earl of Mulgrave (Adriel), the Marquis of Halifax (Jotham), Laurence Hyde (Hushai), Sir Edward Seymour (Amiel).

817. **Barzillai.** James Butler, successively Earl, Marquis, and Duke of Ormond, was born October 19th, 1610. All his life he was a staunch and devoted servant of the house of Stuart ; his first services were under Wentworth, afterwards Earl of Strafford. Even his enemies acknowledged his ability and honesty in the government of Ireland, of which country he was four times lord-lieutenant, namely, from 1642 to 1647, 1648 to 1650, 1662 to 1669, and from 1677 to 1685. He accompanied Charles II. during his exile, zealously serving him during the time of his misfortunes on many important occasions. In the profligate Court of his royal master he was insulted by the king's favourites, particularly by Buckingham, who is said to have incited the notorious Captain Blood to assassinate him. His unswerving fidelity, stern integrity, and immaculate virtue seem to have overawed Charles, who knew the value of such a servant, though he had

little in common with his character.   Ormond's loyalty is sufficiently attested by Charles II. himself.   "I have done," he once said, "everything to disoblige that man, but it is not in my power to make him my enemy" (Hume, *Hist. of England*, vol. viii. p. 154).   He died July 21st, 1688.   For Ormond's biography, see Carte's voluminous Life ; for his character, *Continuation of the Life of Clarendon*, p. 4 (fol. edit.), and Burnet's *Own Time*, vol. i. p. 230.

825. **The court he practised.**   A curious zeugma ; in applying the word practise to ' the court' Dryden appears to be using the word in the French sense, *pratiquer*, to have intercourse or association with, here it may mean 'to frequent.'   The Century Dictionary quotes Lister, *Journey to Paris*, p. 12, "After having practised the Paris coaches for four months I once rid," etc.   For these harsh Gallicisms, see note on 461 *supra*.

829. **His bed could** once.   Ormond was the father of eight sons and two daughters, and of these eight sons six were dead.

831. **His** eldest **hope**, Thomas, Earl of Ossory.   He was a refined, cultivated, and gallant young soldier, who greatly distinguished himself in the first Dutch war under Sir Edward Spragg ; and in the second Dutch war, in 1673, he was Rear-Admiral of the Blue.   He also served under the Prince of Orange against the French in 1678, greatly distinguishing himself at the Battle of St. Denis.   He died of a fever, July 30th, 1680, just as he had entered on his forty-seventh year.   When some friends were trying to console his father in this great loss he nobly said, "Since I have borne the death of my king I can support that of my child.   I would rather have my dead son than any living son in Christendom."

832. **By me ... always mourned.**   Adapted from Virgil
" Quem semper acerbum,
Semper honoratum, sic Di voluistis, habebo."—*Æn*. v. 49.

843. **haughty Pharaoh**, Louis XIV.   The reference is to the campaign of 1678, but Dryden has exaggerated.

844. **Oh ancient honour.**   Another reminiscence of Virgil
" Heu pietas, heu prisca fides, invictaque bello
Dextera."—*Æn*. vi. 879-80.

864. **Zadoc**, William Sancroft, created Archbishop of Canterbury in January, 1677-8, very unexpectedly.   He was a singularly modest and retiring man, in spite of Burnet's malignant account of him.   See Dr. Oyly's *Life of Sancroft*, p. 319.

866. **Sagan of Jerusalem**, Henry Compton, preferred to the Bishopric of Oxford in December, 1674, and a year afterwards translated to London.   He was the youngest son of Spencer Compton, second Earl of Northampton, hence ' his noble stem.'

868. **Him of the western dome**, John Dolben, successively Canon of Christ Church, Archdeacon of London, Dean of Westminster, and in 1666 Bishop of Rochester. He was translated to York in August, 1683. The western dome is Westminster Abbey, the Prophet's. sons the Westminster boys. He was celebrated as an eloquent preacher : three of his sermons are extant, but hardly support his reputation.

877. **Sharp-judging Adriel**, John Sheffield, Earl of Mulgrave, and afterwards Marquis of Normanby and Duke of Buckinghamshire. He was the Muse's friend, for he posed as the patron of poets, and was a patron of Dryden's, who inscribed *Aurengzebe* to him, as well as the translation of the *Æneid*. ' A muse himself,' as the author of the *Essay on Satire*, in which he was no doubt assisted by Dryden, as a co-translator with Dryden of Ovid's Epistle from Helen to Paris, and as the author of a volume of poems " so middling bad were better." See for an account of his literary productions Johnson's Memoir of him in *The Lives of the Poets*. He was all his life a staunch and consistent Tory. He died in 1720, and was buried in Westminster Abbey ; a singularly touching and interesting epitaph written by himself is inscribed on his monument.

881. **disobedient son were torn.** When in 1679 Monmouth displeased the King by refusing to quit England he was deprived of his offices and honours, and among them of the Lord-Lieutenancy of the East Riding of Yorkshire, and the Governorship of Hull, which were conferred on Mulgrave.

882. **Jotham of piercing wit.** George Savile, successively Viscount, Earl, and Marquis of Halifax, was one of the most active, brilliant, and accomplished statesmen of the 17th century. From 1668, in which he sat on the committee for the examination of the accounts of the money given for the Dutch war, he filled a prominent place in public life. Greatly disliked by the Duke of York, he was, for a time, in favour of the popular party, and favoured the Exclusion Bill, but on its discussion in the House of Lords he opposed it, and its defeat was mainly owing to his eloquence. He was the leader and instructor of a small party called the ' Trimmers,' who professed to be neither Whigs nor Tories, but to avoid the extremes of both factions. His *Character of a Trimmer, Advice to a Daughter, Anatomy of an Equivalent,* and *Maxims of State*, still remain to testify to his "piercing wit and pregnant thought." See Macaulay's admirable account of him (*Hist.* vol. i. pp. 116, 7), and Sir James Mackintosh (*Hist. of the Revolution*, vol. ii. pp. 181, 2).

888. **Hushai, the friend of David,** Laurence Hyde, second son of the Lord Chancellor Clarendon. In 1680 he was created Viscount Hyde, and in 1682 Earl of Rochester. One of the plenipotentiaries at the Treaty of Nimeguen, and for a time

Ambassador in Holland, he was appointed in 1679 one of the Commissioners of the Treasury, and very soon became one of the leading ministers of his age. "He was," says Macaulay, "a consistent, dogged, and rancorous party man, a Cavalier of the old school, a zealous champion of the Crown and of the Church" (*Hist.* vol. i. p. 121). Dryden has not exaggerated his abilities or misrepresented the part he played. He afterwards dedicated to him *The Duke of Guise* and *Cleomenes*.

899. **Amiel**, Edward Seymour, of Berry Pomeroy Castle, the head of the illustrious house of Somerset, the then Duke being descended from a younger branch. He was Speaker of the House of Commons from 1673 to 1679. But in that year, though he was re-elected by the House, he was not accepted by the King. "He was," says Macaulay, "one of the most skilful debaters and men of business in the kingdom," and had "studied all the rules and usages of the House, and thoroughly understood its peculiar temper" (*Hist.* vol. i. p. 243). At this time, though influential and wealthy, he had no title, but he succeeded to a baronetcy in 1688 He was one of those who heartily opposed the Exclusion Bill and supported the Court party.

910. **like the unequal ruler.** The reference is to Phaeton and to Ovid's description of his luckless adventure, *Metam.* ii. 200 *seqq.*

920. **to plume the regal rights.** "To pluck out the regal rights like the feathers of a bird. This use of the word is peculiar. Dryden elsewhere uses it in the sense of to strip by plucking—

One whom, instead of banishing a day,
You should have plum'd of all his borrowed honours."
Maiden Queen, Act ii. Sc. 1 [Christie].

932. **That Shimei.** See note on 585.

939. **Thus long have I.** Malone in his *Life of Dryden* (p. 154) is disposed to believe the statement recorded by Spence in his *Anecdotes* that Charles II. requested Dryden to turn into verse part of the speech made by him, the King, at the Oxford Parliament, and insert it in *Absalom and Achitophel*. Malone has selected the passages in the speech which have their parallel in David's speech, but they do not bear out the statement. It is quite clear that, in spite of some coincidences, Dryden's peroration is not a paraphrase of the King's speech.

957. **But oh that yet.** This line, and the three which follow, were inserted in the second edition.

965. **Gulled.** To 'gull' is to cheat, trick, or defraud. It is a metaphor from the helplessness of a young unfledged bird, analogous to the French *niais*, a nestling, which is used as synonymous with a simpleton.

966. **supplant**, literally to trip up the heels (Lat. *sub* and *planta*). Then it came to mean to displace by stratagem. Cf. for the first sense Milton, *Par. Lost*, x.

> " His legs entwining
> Each other, till *supplanted* down he fell."

For the second, Shakespeare, *Titus Andronicus*

> " And so *supplant* us for ingratitude."

967. **The people's brave.** See note on *Medal*, line 129.

982. **But Esau's hands.** The reference is to *Genesis*, xxvii. 22, and the meaning is that though they pretend to petition me humbly and deferentially, they are practically employing force.

987. **Unsatiate as the barren womb.** Borrowed from *Proverbs*, xxx. 15, 16, "There are three things that are never satisfied, yea, four things say not, it is enough: the grave; and the barren womb; the earth that is not filled with water; and the fire that saith not, It is enough."

1007, 8. **to look on Grace, Her hinder parts.** There are two ways of taking this passage; if the comma after ' Grace ' be retained, as in the first two editions of the poem, then ' her hinder parts' must be in apposition to Law in line 1006, and it must mean that Grace is the ' hinder part of Law'; if the comma after Grace be removed, as it is in the sixth and seventh editions, then it will mean Grace—her hinder parts, *i.e.* Grace's hinder parts. The first meaning is intelligible, the second not. The meaning is that Law is as terrible to look on as the face of God would have been to Moses, and as Moses was permitted to see only the back of God, or otherwise he could not have lived, so up to the present time these people had been permitted to see only the hinder part of Law, *i.e.* Grace, now they shall behold her face—and perish. The reference is of course to *Exodus*, xxxiii. 20-3. See a reference to the same in the *Astræa Redux*.

1011. **artificers of death**, from Ovid, *De Arte Amandi*, i. 655, ' Necis Artifices.'

1026, 7, **nodding, gave consent ... peals of thunder.** A curious illustration of the pseudo-classicism, in which the poets of our ' classical age' delighted. The peal of thunder was with the Greek and Roman epic poets the symbol that prayer was heard and granted.

1028, 9. **a series of new time ... procession ran.** Reminiscences of Virgil, *Eclogue*, iv. 5 and 12.

SECOND PART OF ABSALOM AND ACHITOPHEL.

THE success of *Absalom and Achitophel* had been so great that Dryden was strongly urged to follow it up with a second part sketching the minor characters of the great political drama. This task, however, he declined to undertake. It was undertaken, and it is said at his instigation, by Nahum Tate. Tate is now chiefly known as the coadjutor of Brady in the composition of that detestable version of the Psalms which was long appended to our *Book of Common Prayer*. He was acquainted with Dryden and had addressed to him a complimentary copy of verses on *Absalom and Achitophel* which had appeared, with two others by Duke and Lee, in the second edition. Tate was then pushing his way as a man of letters in London and was not slow to embrace so favourable an opportunity for bringing himself into prominence. With the assistance of Dryden, who is said to have revised the poem, he set to work, and the *Second Part of Absalom and Achitophel* appeared in November, 1682, exactly a year after the First. If Dryden revised the poem, and his vigorous hand is occasionally discernible, he could not counteract the effect of poor Tate's insufferable mediocrity. Dull, nerveless, and feeble, the poem would long since have sunk into oblivion had it not been for the two hundred and fifty lines inserted by Dryden. These lines not only deserve a place but occupy a very high place in his satirical writings, and on these lines, and on these lines only, is full commentary necessary. As no reader could desire to study critically what belongs not to Dryden but to Tate the notes are made as brief as possible, designed merely to elucidate historical references.

38. **And guilty Jebusites.** It was commonly asserted by the Whigs that Charles II. protected the Roman Catholics, whereas so far from protecting them he never prevented the execution of Stafford, Coleman, and others, though they all died asserting solemnly that they had had no part in the Popish Plot.

48. **pampered Corah.** See note on line 632 of First Part.

51. **Michal.** The Queen accused by Oates of being an accomplice in the plot against the King's life.

69. **the pest.** The Plague of 1665.

71. **wars of Tyre ... avenging fire.** The Dutch Wars and the Fire of London.

79. **a guard on modest Corah.** Cf. North's *Examen*, p. 205, " He (Oates) was now in his trine exaltation. . . . He walked about with his guards assigned for fear of the Papists murdering him."

88. deponent's loss. " Oates would never tell all he knew, but always reserved some part of his evidence that he might adapt it to circumstances," see Scott's *Note*. With this description of Oates' position should be compared Lingard, xii. 129-165.

121. too foul to be excused. The Tories habitually asserted that Shaftesbury shared in the concoction of the Popish Plot, of which, however, there is no proof ; nor is it likely. " But," as Scott observes, " we can easily believe the truth of what he is alleged to have said, that ' whoever started the game he had the full advantage of the chase.' "

165. The crown's true heir. This and the following lines are a feeble paraphrase of lines 441-446 in the First Part.

178. Against his orders. An allusion to Monmouth's return from Holland without the King's permission, in November, 1679.

189. Who reach lay hold. This obscurely condensed line appears to mean—those who reach out for a crown and miss it lay hold on Death.

190. Did you for this. The five lines which follow are borrowed from the First Part, lines 688-9 and 729-734.

216. quashed each penal law etc. Shaftesbury was strongly in favour of the Declaration of Indulgence.

223. shut the royal store. The closing of the Exchequer in Jan., 1672, for which, however, as Mr. Christie has shown, Shaftesbury was not responsible.

226. triple covenant. See note on line 175, First Part.

229. sent our levied powers. The allusion to the union with France against Holland in March, 1672.

280. extorting Ishban, Sir Robert Clayton, Alderman of London and a zealous Whig. He had the reputation of being a greedy usurer.

298. railing Rabsheka, Sir Thomas Player, Chamberlain of the City of London, and one of the city members. In the Oxford Parliament he made a violent speech upon Fitz-Harris being withdrawn from the city jail. Dryden's hand seems discernible in this coarse and vigorous philippic.

310. Next these. Here Dryden's portion commences.

321. Judas, Robert Ferguson, the arch-plotter. He is described by Macaulay as " violent, malignant, regardless of truth, insatiable of notoriety, delighting in intrigue, in tumult, in mischief for its own sake. He toiled during many years in the darkest mines of faction " (*Hist.* vol. i. p. 252). He had been an Independent preacher, and master of an academy which the Dissenters had set up at Islington as a rival to Westminster School and the Charter-house. He was paymaster and manager of the pamphlet press for the party of Monmouth and Shaftesbury.

331. Phaleg, James Forbes, a Scotchman. He had been travelling tutor to the Earl of Derby whom he had accompanied to Paris. A tall, slim man in person, he was in character, according to Carte, the very opposite of what Dryden describes him as being. This is at once the coarsest and most unwarrantably calumnious of Dryden's satirical portraits.

336. that buzzing insect. The reference is to Æsop's well-known fable.

353. Ben Jochanan, the Rev. Samuel Johnson. Born in 1649 in Warwickshire, and educated at Trinity College, Cambridge, he was in 1669 ordained and presented with the rectory of Corringham in Essex. But about 1678 he came up to London, got acquainted with the leaders of the Whig party, and became in 1679 domestic chaplain to Lord William Russell. After suffering many indignities and calamities in consequence of his liberal opinions, he died in May, 1703. "I do not know," said Coleridge (*Table Talk*, p. 208), "where I could put my hand upon a book containing so much sense and sound constitutional doctrine as this thin folio of Johnson's works."

371. He chose the Apostate. The object of Johnson's work on Julian the Apostate was to institute a tacit comparison between Julian and the Duke of York, and, in describing and justifying the animosity of the Christians against Julian, he justifies by implication the animosity of the Whigs against the Duke of York. He quotes with approval the furious invectives of St. Gregory and St. Chrysostom, citing at the same time the testimony of Libanius that Julian was killed by a Christian, which comes perilously near approval of the assassination of the Duke.

385. The son that showed, the reference is to Ham exposing Noah (*Genesis*, ix. 22).

392, 3. thy hot father ... of a sect. Dryden is here turning the tables on Johnson. I think, he says, that the Apostate was after all a better man than these rancorous fathers of the Church, that it was they who in their unchristian spite and acrimony belonged not to the 'Mother Church,' but 'to a sect.' 'Thy hot father' may mean either St. Gregory or St. Chrysostom, one of whom pronounced Julian to 'be a traitor next to Judas,' and the other asserted that he was 'in Hell undergoing endless punishment.'

396. Balak, the famous Dr. Gilbert Burnet, at this time preacher at the Rolls Chapel and Lecturer at St. Clement's Danes, one of the most prominent figures among the Whig ecclesiastics of the 17th century, and subsequently (1689) Bishop of Salisbury. Of his voluminous writings, his *Lives* and his *History of his own Time* are the most valuable. Dryden again satirized him in the coarsest and most virulent terms in the *Hind* *and Panther,* Part iii. 1140-1205 ; and the Bishop repaid his assailant by describing him in his Memoirs as "a monster of immodesty and impurity of all sorts."

403. **David's psalms translated,** the old version of Sternhold and Hopkins, which was superseded by that of Tate and Brady.

405. **lame Mephibosheth,** Samuel Pordage, the son of a Rev. John Pordage, rector of Bradfield in Berkshire, who in 1654 was deprived of his living on a charge of conversation with evil spirits. This wretched poetaster, who in Oldham's imitation of Juvenal's third Satire is substituted for Codrus, was on the Whig side, and had twice attacked Dryden, once in *Azariah and Hushai,* which was a scurrilous reply to *Absalom and Achitophel,* and again in *The Medal Reversed,* a reply to *The Medal* For the lameness of Mephibosheth, see ii. *Sam.* x. 13.

407. **rotten Uzza,** a very obscure allusion. In Jacob Tonson's key to *Absalom and Achitophel,* published in 1716, the initials J. H. are given as those of the person intended, and in the *State Poems,* vol. iii. p. 367, there is an allusion under the same initials :—

> " J. H. sets up as one of sense
> Does for a poet stand
> . . . . .
> He who was reckon'd the buffoon
> In former Parliaments.

In Mulgrave's *Essay on Satire* the full name is given, "Till he takes Huett and Jack Hall for wits," so this person was some small wit of the time. Mr. Christie thinks that they refer to John Hall, whose name appears as one of the contributors to the *Lacrymæ Musarum*—the collection of poems written on the occasion of Lord Hastings' death—among which Dryden's first poem was printed, but this Hall died in 1656.

408. **Doeg,** Elkanah Settle. There had been an old feud between Dryden and Settle—see biography of Dryden at the beginning of this volume—but Settle probably appears here because of his connection with the Whigs, whom he had joined in 1680, because of his pamphlet entitled *The Character of a Popish Successor,* and because of his recent reply to *Absalom and Achitophel,* in a poem called *Absalom Senior, or Achitophel Transprosed.* He was now 'City Poet,' and for a description of him in this capacity and in that of Superintendent of Pope-burnings, see Otway's *Poet's Complaint,* stanzas viii. and xi.

413. **blundering kind of melody.** With Dryden's general account of Settle's style given here may be compared his prose criticism in his *Remarks upon the Empress of Morocco,* written in conjunction with Crowne and Shadwell :— " He is an animal of a most deplored understanding. His being is on a twilight of

sense and some glimmering of thought which he can never fashion into wit or English. His style is boisterous and rough-hewn, his rhyme incorrigibly lewd, and his numbers perpetually harsh and ill-sounding.

419. **But faggoted his notions.** It is curious to find that Dryden appears to have been indebted for this image to Flecknoe, "For his learning 'tis all capping verses and *faggoting* poets' *loose lines* which fell from him as disorderly as faggot sticks when the band is broke" (Flecknoe's *Enigmatical Characters* (1658), p. 77). See Malone's *Life of Dryden*, p. 170.

424. **All his occasions.** The justice of Dryden's satire is shown by Settle's political career. In 1679 he was a Tory, in 1680 a Whig, in 1683 a Tory again.

444. **to transprose**, the reference is to the title of Settle's poem, *Achitophel Transprosed*.

446. **Who makes heaven's gate** refers to the opening couplet of Settle's poem :—

" In gloomy times, when priestcraft bore the sway,
And made heaven's gate a lock to their own key."

451. **In fire-works.** The ceremony of burning the effigy of the Pope amid fireworks on the 17th of November, 1680, had been entrusted to Settle, and since then he had been generally employed in business of this kind. Poor Settle, whose work as a poet is correctly estimated in Dryden's Satire, not long after this sank very low. He was reduced to attend a booth in Bartholomew Fair, where he was hired to exhibit puppets, and in a farce called *St. George for England* he acted as a dragon enclosed in a case of green leather. Young refers to this in his *First Epistle to Pope*—

" Poor Elkenah, all other charges past,
For bread in Smithfield dragons hiss'd at last."

Pope refers to the same thing (*Dunciad*, 285-90), representing the ghost of Settle as initiating the King in the mysteries of the realm of dulness. Settle died in Feb., 1723-4, a pensioner of the Charter-house. He was the author of nineteen dramas and innumerable poems, all worthless and all now forgotten.

459. **Og**, Thomas Shadwell. See for commentary Introduction and Notes to *Mac Flecknoe*.

482. **Eat opium.** Shadwell's addiction to opium was well known, and according to one tradition it was an overdose of it which caused his death.

524. **See where involved.** This is a description of the Whig King's Head Club, which met at the King's Head Tavern, near

Temple Bar. They called themselves the Green Ribbon Club, because the members wore a green ribbon in opposition to the Tories, who wore in their hats a scarlet ribbon.

535. **Industrious Arod**, Sir William Waller, son of the famous Parliamentary general. He had made himself very conspicuous in investigating the Popish Plot, and in hunting the Papists. With the assistance of Captain Dangerfield he had exposed the Meal Tub Plot, and by getting information out of a midwife of the name of Collier he had exposed also Fitz-Harris's Plot. " He was," says Roger North, " a great inquisitor of priests and Jesuits, and Gutter (as the term was) of Popish Chapels. In which he proceeded with that scandalous rigour as to bring forth the pictures and other furniture of great value and burn them publicly : which gave occasion to suspect, and some said posi-tively that, under this pretence, he kept the good things for him-self " (*Examen*, p. 277).

555. **Zaken**, member of Parliament. He had been an unsuc-cessful candidate in 1679.

571. **From Egypt ... a guardian**, a bold reference to the King's relations with France.

576. **rights to violate**. It was a common device for the Whigs to refuse supplies when dissatisfied with the Court. Scott quotes a paper of instructions issued by the Whig constituents to their representatives in 1680, praying " that they would still literally pursue the same measures and grant no supplies to the Crown till they saw themselves effectually secured from Popery and arbitrary power."

597. **wars of Tyre**, Dutch wars. The whole of the passage describing the Duke's retirement is an excellent example of the ' forcible-feeble ' in rhetoric.

599. **quits the promised land**. When the excitement of the Popish Plot was at its height the King, by the advice of Danby, requested the Duke of York to leave England for a while. Accordingly the Duke retired to Brussels. See the King's letter or order (dated Feb. 28th, 1678-9) in Scott's note.

733. **Then Justice wake**. In this line and to line 746 Dryden's hand is plainly discernible.

749. **bribed with Egypt's gold**. If the King was in the pay of France, of the incredible corruptions of many of the so-called patriots there can be no doubt. Lord Russell, Algernon Sydney, Sir Thomas Lyttelton, Garraway, Hampden, Powle, Sacheverell, Foley, were all in receipt of bribes. See Hallam, *Const. Hist.* vol. ii. p. 406-9. For full details see Appendix to Dalrymple's *Memoirs*, pp. 316-9.

793. **From Hebron ... returned**. See note on line 59, First Part.

Scott says that the presence of the Duke of York in Scotland was "very acceptable to the nobles and gentry," but the Covenanters would have told a very different tale. In the account in the text we must remember that a Tory and an apologist for the Tories is speaking.

805. **Through Sion's streets.** The Duke of York returned from Scotland to London in April, 1682.

811. **Jothran,** George Legge, created Earl of Dartmouth in 1682. He was the son of Colonel William Legge, so eminently distinguished by his loyal attachment both to Charles I. and to Charles II. He had served in both the Dutch wars, was an admiral, and at this time Master of the Ordnance. He was one of the few really honest and consistent public men of his time. He afterwards commanded the fleet sent out to oppose William of Orange. At the Revolution he was thrown into the Tower, where he died in October, 1691.

819. **Benaiah,** General Edward Sackville. The reference is to his gallant services at Tangier. He had spoken very contemptuously of those who had concocted and of those who believed in the Popish Plot, and had been expelled from the House of Commons in consequence.

825. **While those that sought.** Scott says that in a MS. note of Narcissus Luttrel's it is said that the Earl of Anglesea is specially glanced at. With these lines compare Dryden's *Prologue to the Duke of York on his Return from Scotland,* 14-27.

835. **forced ... yield.** The omission of 'to' before the infinite is not uncommon in the poetry of the 17th century. Cf. Milton, *Par. Reg.* iv. 409, 10—
> "Either tropic now
> 'Gan thunder."

Mr. Christie quotes *Hudibras,* Part I. 2, verse 1111
> "But force it take an oath before."

885. **Absalom.** See note on line 18, Part I.

913-8. **Festival instals ... Dashing ... mirth.** Shaftesbury, Monmouth, and the leaders of their party had arranged to hold a great gathering of 'loyal Protestants' in the city, in opposition to a meeting invited by the Artillery Company to dine with the Duke of York at Merchant-Taylors Hall, April 21st, 1682, but on the 19th of April a Royal Proclamation was issued forbidding the meeting and banquet. See Scott's note for particulars.

938. **laurelled Asaph,** Dryden.

941. **Bezaliel,** the Duke of Beaufort, President of Wales.

943. **Knites' rocky province,** Wales.

958. **copied in his son**, Charles, Marquis of Worcester; he died before his father in July, 1698.

967. **Abdael**, Christopher, Duke of Albemarle, the son of General Monk. Some of his contemporaries describe him as unusually dull and stupid. He was Chancellor of the University of Cambridge in 1682, hence the prophets' school. The frigid bombast of Tate's fulsome rubbish is worthy alike of the flattered and the flatterer.

985. **Eliab**, Henry Bennet, Earl of Arlington, the celebrated minister, Secretary of State in the Cabal Administration, and afterwards Lord Chamberlain. He died in July, 1685. See Macaulay's character of him (*Hist.* vol. i. 101, 2).

994. **young Othniel's bride.** Lady Isabella Bennet, the only daughter and heiress of Arlington, married Henry Fitzroy, Duke of Grafton, second son of Charles II., by Barbara Palmer, Duchess of Cleveland.

1003. **Helon**, Louis Duras, Earl of Feversham, a Frenchman, and a Protestant, being of Huguenot descent. He afterwards distinguished himself by his cowardice and incompetence in the campaign against Monmouth.

1013. **Amri**, Sir Heneage Finch, Earl of Winchelsea and Lord Chancellor. He succeeded Shaftesbury as Lord Keeper. He was one of the most eminent of English lawyers.

1025. **Sheva**, Sir Roger L'Estrange, one of the fathers of English journalism, born December, 1616, after the Restoration. He became a rancorous and intemperate Tory, the champion (on paper) of the Church and the Court. He was the editor of two papers, *The Observator*, 1679-1687; *The Heraclitus Ridens*, and of several others. For many years he was Licenser of the Press. He died in September, 1704.

1036. **Advanced his signal.** The reference is to the brazen serpent set up by Moses, which stayed the plague of serpents (*Numbers*, xxi.).

1039. **What tribute.** From this point we see poor Tate on his unsupported pinions, on which he soars and croaks to the end of the poem.

1067. **Who now sails off.** The Duke of York's voyage to Scotland in May, 1682, to bring back the Duchess, 'his beauteous dear,' is the subject of this wretched stuff.

1084. **treacherous sands ... devour.** The Duke's ship struck upon a bank, the Lemmon Ore; he managed, with a few attendants, to get off in a boat, leaving all the rest to their fate, among them the Earl of Roxburghe, Hyde, one of the sons of the great Earl of Clarendon, the Lord O'Brien, about 300 seamen, and the rest of his retinue.

1100. **Urania, the Duchess of York,.** so named from the Uranian Venus.

1123. **Hyblæan swarms.** See note on line 697 of First Part.

1131. **Ziloah,** Sir John Moore, the Tory Lord Mayor, the ' loyal head ' of line 181 in *The Medal.*

1132. **Surges.** To discuss the various readings in Tate's trash would be absurd, but we may notice that *syrtes*, quicksands, is one of the variants here.

1133, 4. **A viler pair Than Ziph or Shimei.** The viler pair are Pilkington and Shute, the Whig sheriffs, who are the ' two gouty hands ' of line 181 of *The Medal.* Ziph is Richard Cornish, one of the sheriffs in the preceding year. For Shimei see note on line 598 of First Part.

1135. **Ziloah's loyal labours.** In September, 1682, the Lord Mayor Moore contrived, by the most unwarrantable means, to procure, with the assistance of the Court party, the election of two Tory sheriffs, North and Rich. This was followed by the election of a Tory Lord Mayor to succeed Moore. A Tory reaction had for some time been setting in, and this was the climax, for it both marked and restored Tory ascendancy in the very stronghold of Whiggism, and so from the Tory point of view Israel's peace was restored. Not long after this Shaftesbury fled to Holland.

THE MEDAL.

SCARCELY had the First Part of *Absalom and Achitophel* made its appearance when the bill of high treason against Shaftesbury was presented to the Grand Jury. It was ignored (November 24th, 1681) and Shaftesbury was immediately liberated from the Tower. The joy of the Whigs knew no bounds. A medal was struck bearing the head and name of the popular hero ; and on the reverse was represented a sun, obscured with a cloud, rising over the Tower and the City of London, with the date of the rejection of the bill, and the motto *Lœtamur.* Impressions of this medal were distributed among the Whigs, and, much to the chagrin of the Tories, all good Whigs took care to wear the ornament ostentatiously displayed on their bosoms. A priest, whom Spence met at Pope's house, gave the following account of the origin of Dryden's poem—" It was Charles II. who gave Mr. Dryden the hint for writing his poem called the Medal. One day as the King was walking in the Mall, and talking with Dryden he said, ' If I was a poet (and I think I am poor enough to be one) I would write a poem on such a subject in the following manner,' and then gave him the plan for it. Dryden took the hint and carried the poem as soon as it was written to the King, and had a present of a hundred broad pieces for it" (Spence's *Anecdotes*, Edit. Singer, p. 129). However this may be, the poem was published at the beginning of March, 1682.

EPISTLE TO THE WHIGS.

P. 68, ll. 11, 2. **a poor Polander.** Shaftesbury was bantered by his contemporaries for aspiring to the crown of Poland when John Sobieski was elected in 1675. See a pamphlet entitled " A Modest Vindication of the Earl of Shaftesbury in a Letter to a Friend concerning his being Elected King of Poland." It was indeed the stock joke against him—allusions to it abound in the satirical literature of that time.

l. 18. **to B.** William Bower, the engraver of the medal.

P. 69, l. 7. **Preface to the "No Protestant Plot."** The reference is to a tract in three parts which was written to prove the innocence of Shaftesbury, College, and the Whigs from the alleged intrigues against the King at Oxford. The first part was attributed to Shaftesbury himself, the two last to Ferguson, the Judas of line 321 of Second Part of *Absalom and Achitophel*.

l. 14. **Scanderberg.** The famous Albanian chief and enemy to the Turks, George Castriota, born in 1404, died at Lissa in 1467. On the taking of Lissa, where his remains were discovered, the Turks are said to have dug up his bones and converted them into amulets under the impression that the bones would transfer his courage to those who wore the amulets. Cf. *State Poems*, vol. i. 190—

" Let it, like bones of Scanderberg, incite."

P. 70, l. 7. **petition in a crowd.** An allusion to the Act passed in 1661 which prohibits the presentation of any petition to the King or Houses of Parliament "accompanied with excessive numbers of people, nor at any time with above the number of ten persons."

l. 19. **dead author's pamphlet,** the celebrated Andrew Marvel, the poet and Puritan controversalist, born at Hull in 1620, died in London in 1678. The reference is to his *Account of the Growth of Popery and Arbitrary Government in England*, published in 1678.

l. 21. **Buchanan,** the famous George Buchanan, the tutor of Mary Queen of Scots. The work Dryden refers to is a noble plea for civil liberty—for limited as distinguished from autocratic monarchy.

l. 30. **Theodore Beza**, one of the chief promoters of the Protestant Reformation (born at Vezelai in 1519) and a central figure in the great religious controversies of the sixteenth century. He died in October, 1605.

l. 15. **writ the "Whip and Key."** *A Whip for the Fool's Back* was one of the many replies to *Absalom and Achitophel*: it was written by a Nonconformist minister whose name is not known, and who was also the author of *A Key with the Whip to open the Mystery and Iniquity of the Poem called Absalom and Achitophel*.

l. 28. **brother of Achitophel**, the writer of the pamphlet just referred to. Achitophel has just been explained as 'the brother of a fool,' so Dryden's sarcasm is obvious.

P. 73, l. 2. **saucy Jack.** Jack is commonly used by the Elizabethan writers for an upstart or flippant fribble. Cf. *Richard III.* Act i. Sc. 3—

" Since every Jack became a gentleman
There's many a gentle person made a Jack."

So also in *Much Ado,* Act i. Sc. 1, "Do you play the flouting Jack."

---

2. **English idiots.** The word idiot is directly from the Greek, ἰδιώτης, a private person, hence one who is inexperienced or uneducated, so silly, foolish. Cf. the history of *lewd*.

15. **Polish is Rejoice.** *I.e.* in the language of Shaftesbury and his partizans scoffingly called Poles with reference to Shaftesbury's alleged Polish aspirations.

26. **A martial hero first.** For a commentary on these lines see the life of Shaftesbury at the end of the Introduction.

27. **a pigmy.** See note on line 157 of First Part of *Absalom and Achitophel*.

32. **for sums of gold.** Shaftesbury was a member of the Council of State appointed, after the dissolution of the Rump Parliament, in July, 1653. The members had a salary of £1000, but Mr. Christie has shown that Shaftesbury received no salary.

33. **cast himself ... saint-like mould.** There is no proof that Shaftesbury affected the sanctimonious piety of the Puritans, but as he undoubtedly "held a concert with the Anti-Monarchists and Fanatics" (North, *Examen*, p. 41) when he belonged to that party, there is some colour for Dryden's rhetoric.

41. **interlope**, to run between, to intercept the trade or traffic of a company, so to traffic without a proper license; from the Latin *inter* and the Dutch *loopen*, to run.

52. **malice reconciled ... Prince.** Dryden is here accounting for the reasons which induced Shaftesbury to quit the side of the Parliament and join the King, which he did when, in the spring of 1660, he was one of the Commissioners who went to Breda.

54. **Rewarded faster.** In 1661 he was made Baron Ashley, Chancellor of the Exchequer and Under Treasurer ; in April, 1672, Earl of Shaftesbury, and in November, Lord Chancellor.

60. **lawful gears.** Gear properly means dress, harness or tackle, then dress or ornament, and is derived from the Anglo-Saxon *gearwe*. It may here be a metaphor from running in traces or in harness, with the collateral notion of ornaments or honours.

65. **loosed our triple hold.** See note on *Absalom and Achitophel*, l. 175.

73. **So Samson**, the reference is to Samson and Delilah (*Judges*, xvii. 17-19).

75. **this fatal counsel.** It was by the advice of Shaftesbury that the King issued the Declaration of Indulgence in March, 1672, which was so unpopular that it was afterwards recalled.

78. **seduced to arbitrary sway.** The King, much to the chagrin of Shaftesbury, cancelled the Declaration in March, 1673, and Shaftesbury was so annoyed that he practically broke from the King and the Court party, attached himself to the Whigs, and began his career as a demagogue.

94. **in thy Pindaric way.** To the people of Dryden's age Pindar was supposed to be the representative of wild licence in art, and it was on that assumption that the so-called Pindaric or Irregular Odes were written, the characteristic of which was that the order of the rhymes and the length of the lines could be as the poet pleases. This monstrous line of fourteen syllables is given as an illustration.

96. **Phocion ... Socrates,** Phocion was put to death on a charge of treason in B.C. 317, and Socrates on a charge of impiety in B.C. 399. In both cases the Athenians subsequently acknowledged and lamented the injustice and folly of what they had done.

114. **Inherent right,** the doctrine of the thorough-going Cavaliers and Tories, which found its most extravagant and emphatic expression in Sir Robert Filmer's *Patriarcha*. This work, though written in Charles I.'s reign, had only recently (1680) been published.

119. **new Jehu,** Shaftesbury.

129. **usurping brave.** Brave is the French form of the Italian *bravo*, a braggart villain, a cut-throat. The Italian form is naturalized in English, but the French form is obsolete. Dryden has, however, often used it. Cf. *Absalom and Achitophel*, 967, "The people's *brave*, the politician's fool."

131. **loathe ... manna ... long for quails**, the reference is to the *Book of Numbers*, xi. 4 and 32.

136. **None can they**, note the extent to which Dryden's Toryism was carried.

140. **laws which they dispense.** Cf. the 'divine' maxim, "A Deo rex, a rege lex." See the addresses presented in 1687 from the Middle and Inner Temple to James II.

145. **The man who laughed but** once, Marcus Licinius Crassus, nicknamed Agelastus, because he never laughed (Pliny, *Nat. Hist.* vii. 19). Cicero says (*De Finibus*, v. 30) that he laughed once, and Tertullian (*De Animâ*, lii.) that he died in a fit of laughter, while Lucilius tells us what is here related. "The relation of Lucilius and now become common concerning Crassus ... that he never laughed but once in all his life, and that was at an ass eating thistles, is something strange" (Sir T. Browne, *Vulgar Errors*, Bk. VII. ch. xvi.). Philemon the Comic Poet is said to have died from the same cause at seeing an ass eating figs (*Lucian*, lxii. 25).

146. **mumbling**, to speak indistinctly, or to chew inefficiently. From the Middle English verb *momelen*, to speak indistinctly.

147. **a jury chaw**, now generally spent chew. Middle English *chewen*, from Anglo-Saxon *ceówan*. Christie quotes in illustration :—

> "Like him who chaws
> Sardinian herbage to contract his jaws."
> Dryden's Tr. of Virgil's *Seventh Eclogue*, 60.

The jury referred to is the grand jury who threw out the Bill against Shaftesbury.

149. **The witnesses**, these were the witnesses called against Shaftesbury in support of the charge of high treason ; they were John Booth, Edward Turberville, John Smith, Bryan Haines, John Macnamara, and others who came to corroborate evidence. Some of these scoundrels had been the tools of Shaftesbury, who had indeed brought them over to England to give evidence about a Popish plot in Ireland.

150. **med'cinally good**, to be pronounced as a four-syllabled word, mēd'cĭnāllў. Cf. Milton's *Samson Agonistes*, 626—

> "or mēd'cĭnăl liquor can assuage."

151. **fastened on their festered sore.** They were truthful and trustworthy when they gave evidence in favour of the Popish Plot, were lying and untrustworthy when they gave evidence against their former employer, Shaftesbury, and so 'rogue and saint distinguish'd by their side.'

155. **They rack** even **Scripture.** This is partly a reference to perjury corroborated by the scriptural oath, and partly a reference to the sectary fanatics. Cf. with this attack on them, *Religio Laici*, 400-426, and *Hind and Panther, passim.*

·163· **our oracle,** the church, or possibly the King.

166. **emporium,** a mart ; Greek ἐμπόριον, Lat. emporium. Cf. *Annus Mirabilis*, st. 302, "And while this fam'd emporium we prepare."

180, 1. **The head ... gouty hands.** As Shaftesbury's intrigues appeared to be making a civil war imminent, some of the leading merchants came over to the royal party. The 'head' was Sir John Moore, Lord Mayor in 1681 ; the two gouty hands were the two Whig sheriffs, Thomas Pilkington and Samuel Shute. See *Absalom and Achitophel*, Part II. 1131 and 1134, where Moore appears as Ziloah, and Pilkington and Shute as Ziph and Shimei.

190. **chapmen,** merchants ; Anglo-Saxon, *ceápman.*

216. **Thus, when the heir,** refers to the parable of the vineyard and the husbandmen (*St. Matthew*, xxi. 33-39).

225. **Cyclop-like,** a reference to *Odyssey*, ix. 288-291, where Polyphemus devours six of Ulysses' crew.

227, 8. **Perhaps not wholly ... clip his regal rights.** This verse and the verses which follow describe the 'cypher-like state' of royalty to which Shaftesbury and his party would have wished to reduce the crown. Dryden's remarks find remarkable corroboration in North's *Examen*, p. 119. 'Clip his rights' is a metaphor from clipping coin. Milled coin was not in circulation till 1663, and much of the old hammered coin was still current ; it was easily clipped, and this clipping of the coin was one of the great grievances of Dryden's age. See Macaulay, *Hist.* vol. iv. p. 116.

239. **whet like a Croatian band.** The Croatians in Dryden's time were synonymous with ferocious and predatory barbarians. 'Whet' is properly an active verb, from the Anglo-Saxon *hwettan*, to sharpen, and it means either to sharpen a metal weapon, or to urge on, to incite ; here 'their weapons' must be understood.

255. **But thou** etc. A fine illustration of Dryden's power of rhetorical invective.

269. **stum,** new wine, must, used for fermenting old wine ; from the Dutch, *stom*, new wine. Cf. Addison, "A clammy vapour that arises from the *stum* of grapes when they lie mashed in the vat " etc. (*Travels in Italy*), and cf. *Hudibras*—

> "Drink every letter of 't in *stum*,
> And make it brisk champagne become."

271. formidable cripple. An allusion to certain bodily infirmities from which Shaftesbury suffered, references to which are common in the satires of that age. See *Albion and Albanius*, instruction for the decorations of Act iii. Duke's *Review*, and Mulgrave's *Essay on Satire*, where he is thus described

> " The nimblest creature of the busy kind
> His limbs are crippled and his body shakes,
>
> What gravity can hold from laughing out
> To see him drag his feeble legs about."

283. A conventicle. Accent on the third syllable, as always in Dryden and his contemporaries.

284. Bedlam, the celebrated hospital for lunatics. The form is a corruption from Bethlehem, the hospital of St. Mary of Bethlehem, incorporated by Henry VIII. in 1547 as a royal foundation for the reception of lunatics.

286. Without a vision. The power and skill with which Dryden predicts the result of Shaftesbury's intrigues and policy are as remarkable as the art with which he brings his satire to its climax.

293. The swelling poison. A cruel and disgusting reference to the abscess from which Shaftesbury suffered, and which for several years he had to keep open by a silver pipe.

316. And thrust out Collatine. The reference is to Lucius Tarquinius Collatinus, the husband of Lucretia, and the cousin of Sextus Tarquinius, the ravisher of Lucretia, whose deed of shame led to the expulsion of the Tarquins and the abolition of monarchy in Rome ; the application is to Monmouth. As Collatinus, though he had been instrumental in destroying the Tarquins, yet went into exile because of his relationship to them, so Shaftesbury, who in his intrigues in behalf of Monmouth had inoculated the people with republican ideas, will find that they will thrust out the King he would impose on them.

319. halting vengeance. The 'halting vengeance' was the anarchy into which Shaftesbury and his partizans had plunged the kingdom ; the last lines refer to the reaction which was now plainly setting in in favour of the Court party.

322. Pudet hæc. 'Shameful it is that such scandals as these could have been uttered by you, and could not have been refuted !' The quotation is from Ovid, *Met.* i. 758, and Dryden has altered 'nobis' into 'vobis,' as it is addressed to the Whigs.

MAC FLECKNOE.

AMONG the many replies both in verse and prose elicited by *The Medal* was a satire entitled *The Medal of John Bayes*. In this lampoon, which is distinguished by its scurrility even among the scurrilous libels of Settle, Care, and Pordage, Dryden is charged with gross and infamous crimes, the author adding in the preface that Dryden has not been " hardly dealt with, since he knows and so do all his old acquaintance that there is not one untrue word spoke of him." The writer of this shameful production was Thomas Shadwell. Born in or about 1640, of a good family, at Santon Hall in Norfolk, he had been educated at Cambridge, and afterwards entered at the Middle Temple. He had then commenced wit and play-wright, and in this capacity had come into contact with Dryden. For some time they appear to have been on friendly terms. In 1674 he had, in conjunction with Crowne, assisted Dryden in the Remarks on Settle's *Empress of Morocco*. Nor had their friendly relations been terminated by certain sneering allusions to Dryden's rhyming plays and to the salary he received from the King's Theatre, which Shadwell had made in the Epilogue and Dedication of his *Virtuoso ;* for we find Dryden assisting him two years afterwards with an epilogue. [See Dryden's Epilogue to *The True Widow*.] But the amity which literary jealousies only disturbed or impaired, political differences soon converted into rancorous hostility. Dryden had attached himself to the Tories, Shadwell to the Whigs. In 1682 Shadwell attacked the Anti-Exclusionists in a comedy entitled *The Lancashire Witches, or Teague O'Divelly the Irish Priest,* and the war between the poet of the Tories and the poetaster of the Whigs began in earnest. What immediately inspired *Mac Flecknoe* was *The Medal of John Bayes*. Much of the satire in *Mac Flecknoe* is undoubtedly unjust. Shadwell is, as a comic poet, greatly superior to Dryden. He is anything but dull ; he has what Dryden has not, a rich vein of humour, coarse indeed, but genuine, much real dramatic power both in vivid portraiture and in the presentation of incident. His *Epsom Wells* and his *Squire of Alsatia* give us singularly vivid pictures of the social life of those times. But for the rest he was fair game for the satirist. His habits were sensual and dissolute ; he was fre-quently half-muddled with wine or opium ; he had a foul tongue and a foul pen ; and his absurd affectation of posing as a second Ben Jonson, partly on the strength of his gross and unwieldy person, and partly because of the analogy, not altogether fanciful, between his genius and Ben's, made him the laughing-stock of all who knew him. After the appearance of *Mac Flecknoe* in October, 1682, Shadwell and Dryden lived, to borrow a phrase from Dr.

Johnson, 'in a perpetual reciprocity of malevolence,' and Dryden, as we have seen, attacked Shadwell with still more acrimony in the Second Part of *Absalom and Achitophel*. Mortifying indeed must it have been to him when in August, 1689, Shadwell superseded him in the poet-laureateship. Shadwell died December 6th, 1692, and his dramatic works were printed in 4 vols. in 1720. Nothing could be more happy and ingenious than the plot of *Mac Flecknoe*. In itself inimitable, it became, in turn, the model of a satire even more renowned, for Pope derived from it the idea of the *Dunciad*.

Richard Flecknoe, who is represented as the father and predecessor of Shadwell in the kingdom of dulness, was an Irishman and a Roman Catholic priest. An industrious scribbler for upwards of half a century—his first poem is dated 1626, and he is supposed to have died about 1678—he had gone on producing poems, plays, and prose pieces—

> " Though it were in spite
> Of Nature and his stars to write."

Of his five dramas he could only get one to be acted, and that was damned. He had been the butt of Marvel's satire as early as some time between 1642-1645, between which period Marvel was in Rome. [See for his satire, which is entitled *Fleckno an English Priest at Rome*, his poetical works, Murray's Edit., p. 120 *seqq.*] In the Dedication to *Limberham*, written in 1678, Dryden notices "how natural is the connection between a bad poet and Flecknoe," and it would appear from an ambiguous passage in the same Dedication that Flecknoe had recently died. Dryden selected him to fill the place he fills in this satire not because he had had any quarrel with Flecknoe, but simply because his name had become a synonym for poetaster and dullard. Thus the Earl of Dorset in his satire on Edward Howard writes—

> " These . . . . antipodes to common sense,
> These fools to Flecknoe, pry'thee tell me whence
> Does all this mighty mass of dulness spring";

and Oldham, who, in his imitation of Horace's *Ars Poetica* had spoken respectfully of him, classing him with Cowley, in his satire in the person of Spenser classes him with Pordage, Edward Howard,.and others, who "are damned to wrapping drugs and wares, and curs'd by all their broken stationers." On the whole Flecknoe must be pronounced to be all that Dryden's satire implies ; his five plays are certainly beneath contempt, his epigrams and miscellaneous poems, as a rule, dull and tame, but his prose Enigmatical Characters are not without merit. He was, however, the author of one really beautiful copy of verses which ought, in justice to him, to be quoted—

Still-born Silence ! thou that art
Floodgate of the deeper heart !
Offspring of a heavenly kind,
Frost o' the mouth and thaw o' the mind !
Secrecy's confidant, and he
Who makes religion mystery !
Admiration speaking'st tongue !
Leave, thy desert shades among
Reverend hermits' hallow'd cells,
Where retir'd devotion dwells,
With thy enthusiasms come,
Seize our tongues and strike us dumb."

For favourable notices of Flecknoe see Southey's *Omniana*, vol. i. p. 105, and *Retrospective Review*, vol. v. p. 266.

True blue ... poet. Blue was the colour of the badge assumed by the Tories or Church Party. For the explanation of the title cf. North's *Examen*, p. 321, " They (the Tories) called the adversaries *True Blues* because such were not satisfied to be Protestants, as the Churchmen were, but must be *true* Protestants, implying the others to be false ones, just not Papists."

25. **goodly fabric.** Shadwell's gross and unwieldy person is again ridiculed in the character of Og in Second Part of *Absalom and Achitophel*, and see *infra*, 193-5.

29. **Heywood and Shirley.** Thomas Heywood, one of the most voluminous of the Elizabethan dramatists (died about 1650), who has himself told us that he had " either an entire hand or at least a maine finger in 220 plays," of which 23 are extant. Dryden has not done Heywood justice ; his tragedy *A Woman Killed with Kindness* is one of the most powerful and touching plays which have come down to us from the Elizabethan age ; Charles Lamb has done Heywood no more than justice in calling him " a sort of prose Shakespeare." James Shirley (born 1594, died 1666), a voluminous dramatic poet, the last of the Elizabethan dramatists— " The last of a great race, all of whom spoke nearly the same language and had a set of moral feelings and notions in common " (Lamb, *Specimens of English Dramatic Poets*). His lyric " The Glories of our Birth and State," from his masque, *The Contention of Ajax and Ulysses*, is one of the gems of English lyric poetry.

34. **in Norwich drugget.** Dryden clothes Flecknoe in clothes of the fashion he is said himself to have worn when he first came to London. " I remember," writes a correspondent to the

Gentleman's Magazine for 1745, "John Dryden before he paid court to the great in one uniform clothing of Norwich drugget." It was a rough woollen stuff.

36. **When to King John of Portugal.** This is a reference to the following passage in Flecknoe's *Travels*. Speaking of King John of Portugal he says :—" He no sooner understood of my arrival but he sent for me to Court. . . . The next day he sent for me again where, after some two or three hours tryal of my skill (especially in the compositive part of music, in which his majesty chiefly exceeded) I past Court doctor" (*A Relation of Ten Years Travels* etc., p. 51).

37. **that glorious day.** This evidently refers to some actual incident, but Sir Walter Scott and the commentators have been unable to discover it, and I have not been more successful.

42. **in Epsom blankets.** The reference is to Shadwell's play, *Epsom Wells*. Tossing in blankets was a common form of inflicting humiliating punishment.   See Shadwell's *Sullen Lovers*, Act v., " Such a fellow as he deserves to be tossed in a blanket," and Pope, *Dunciad*, II. 153, 4—

> " What street, what lane but knows
> Our purgings, pumpings, *blanketings*, and blows."

43. **new Arion.** Arion, to save himself from being murdered, is fabled to have thrown himself into the sea, after having so charmed by his strains the song-loving dolphins that one of them carried him on his back to land at Tænarus.

47. **Pissing-alley,** a passage running out of the Strand into Holywell Street.   See Stowe's *Survey of London* and Map, between pp. 108, 9, vol. ii.

48. **Resound from Aston Hall.**   I regret to say, that after much research, I can throw no light on this allusion.   It appears from the *Tixhall Letters*, Part i., p. 60, that Walter, Lord Aston, had a house at the Mulberry Gardens in 1635 which may have continued in the family after his death in 1639 and been known as Aston Hall.   There is an Aston mentioned in the *Essay on Satire* where he is called "dull Aston," and in the *Epistle to Julian* where his worthless ballads are referred to, and it is not unlikely that this Aston is to be identified with Colonel Aston, a friend of Sheffield's (see his *Memoirs*, Works, ii., pp. 8-10).   He was evidently a well-to-do person and a scribbler, and his residence may have been known as Aston Hall, but I can trace no connection between this person and Shadwell.

53. **St. André,** a well-known dancing-master of Dryden's time. Cf. *Limberham*, Act iii. Sc. 1, " All were complete, sir, if St.

André would make steps to them." So Oldham *Imitation of Horace*

"St. André never mov'd with such a grace."

54. **thy own Psyche's rhyme.** Shadwell's rhymed opera *Psyche,* produced in 1675 : the versification is execrable.

57. **Singleton,** John Singleton, a celebrated musician and probably leader of the private band. See Lord Braybrooke and Pepys, vol. v. p. 224, and vol. i. p. 156, for the affront put upon him by the King silencing his band that the French music might be heard instead.

59. **Villerius,** Villerius, Grand Master of the Knights of Malta, is one of the leading characters in Davenant's dramatic opera, *The Siege of Rhodes.* A long lyrical dialogue between Villerius and Solyman had been ridiculed in the *Rehearsal* as a combination of "lute and sword." See Christie's *Note.*

64. **The fair Augusta,** London, so designated in the reign of Theodosius. See Crowne's *Masque of Calisto,* where "Augusta is inclined to fears"; both allusions are to the apprehension caused by the political disturbances.

67. **Barbican it hight,** was or is called. The sole instance in English of a passive verb. Cf. Shakespeare, *Midsum. N. D.,* Act v. Sc. 1, "This griestly beast which by name lion *hight*"; and Dryden's version of the *Cock and the Fox,* 40, 1—

> "The noble chanticleer
> So *hight* her cock."

Barbican was a street in Aldersgate, on the west side of Redcross Street. Its name is derived from the Low Latin *barbicana,* an outwork, through the French *barbacane.*

70. **a Nursery.** A theatre established under letters patent in March, 1664, for the training of boys and girls for the stage. All "obscene, scandalous, or offensive passages" were prohibited, and the performances were to be restricted to "what may consist of harmless and inoffensive delights and recreations." Allusions to it are not uncommon among Dryden's contemporaries who sneered at its decorum. Thus, in the *Rehearsal,* Act ii. Sc. 2, Bayer says, "I am resolved hereafter to lend my thoughts wholly for the service of the Nursery." See too Oldham in his *Spenser's Ghost Satire—*

> "Then slighted by the very Nursery
> Mayest thou at last be forc'd to starve with me."

The site of one 'Nursery' was in Golden Lane, Barbican, and to this Dryden refers ; but there was another institution known as the Nursery in Hatton Garden. See Lord Braybrooke's *Pepys' Diary,* vol. iv., p. 318. The lines, 'where unfledged actors' etc., are another parody from Cowley's *Davideis,* Bk. I., 75-6—

" Beneath the dens where unfledged tempests lie,
And infant minds their tender voices try."

74. **little Maximins.** Maximin is the protagonist in Dryden's drama of *Tyrannic Love; or, The Royal Martyr.*

75. **Great Fletcher,** the celebrated John Fletcher, the coadjutor of Beaumont and one of the most distinguished of the Elizabethan dramatists.

75, 76. **buskins ... socks.** The buskin or high-heeled boot is synonymous with the Greek cothurnus, which was worn by actors when acting tragedy, and so symbolized tragedy, just as the sock or low-heeled light shoe was worn in comedy, and so symbolized comedy. So Gray, *Bard,* 128, " In *buskin'd* measures move," and Milton, *L'Allegro,* 132, " If Jonson's learned *sock* be on."

77. **gentle Simkin.** Derrick says that Simkin " is a character of a cobbler in an interlude," but what interlude he does not say, and no one as yet has succeeded in discovering. In a collection of Drolls and Farces, compiled by Francis Kirkman in 1673, there is one called *The Humours of Simpkin,* Simpkin being a stupid clown who is represented as intriguing with an old man's wife and this may be the interlude to which Derrick refers. For this information I am indebted to Mr. P. A. Daniel.

78. **monument ... minds.** Taken from Davenant—

" This to a structure led, long known to fame,
And call'd *the monument of vanish'd minds.*"
                                    Gondibert, Canto v. stanza 36.

79. **Pure clinches.** A clinch or clench is a pun, or play on words. Dryden in the *Essay on Satire,* commenting on the pun made on *Rex* in Horace, *Sat.* I. vii., calls it " a miserable clinch, in my opinion, for Horace to record."

80. **And Panton.** Nothing is known of him beyond what Derrick has told us, that he was " a celebrated punster."

83. **ancient Decker,** Thomas Decker, the celebrated Elizabethan dramatist, who divided with Heywood the leadership of the Plebeian School, and had a famous controversy with Ben Jonson. Some of his comedies, *The Roaring Girl* and *The Honest Whore,* are in their kind excellent.

87. **worlds of " Misers,"** refers to Shadwell's adaptation of Molière's *L'Avare* under the title of " The Miser."

88. **Humourists ... Hypocrites.** The reference in the first is to Shadwell's comedy, *The Humourists*—the second would seem to refer to some imitation or adaptation of Molière's *Tartuffe;* if Shadwell was concerned in such a work, there is now no trace of it. *Tartuffe* had been adapted in 1670 by Mathew Medbourne under the title of *The French Puritan* and had been received with

'universal applause.' Possibly Shadwell may have intended to recast it for revival. The allusion, if there be any, is lost. Scott conjectures that it may refer to the Irish priest and Tory chaplain in *The Lancashire Witches*, who is, by the way, again introduced in *The Amorous Bigot*.

89. **Raymond ... Bruce**, Raymond, 'a gentleman of wit and humour,' is a character in Shadwell's *Humourists*, and Bruce 'a gentleman of wit and sense,' a character in his *Virtuoso*.

96. **Ogleby**, John Ogleby or Ogilby, a voluminous poetaster and translator, born near Edinburgh in 1600. He published a translation of Virgil in 1649-50, of Æsop in 1651, of the *Iliad* and the *Odyssey* between 1660-5, which, as a boy, Pope admired, but in his mature years he pronounced it to be beneath criticism. In the *Dunciad*, Bk. I. 141, he is called " Ogilby the great." Ogilby died 4th Sept., 1676.

99. **Herringman**, Henry Herringman the. publisher. It was for him Dryden worked when he first came to London, and Herringman continued to publish for him till Tonson became his publisher. Herringman chiefly published poetry and plays, hence his place here.

104, 5. **His brows ... lambent dulness.** The reference is to *Æneid*, II. 680-86, the fiery halo over the head of Iulus, just as ' Rome's other hope ' is a reference to *Æneid*, XII. 168.

106. **As Hannibal.** See *Polybius*, III. ii., and Livy XXI. ch. i.

116. **Love's Kingdom.** Flecknoe's stupid Pastoral-Trage-Comedy.

124. **So Romulus.** Romulus is said to have wished to build Rome on the Palatine, Remus on the Aventine, and it was decided to settle the question by augury ; and on Remus seeing six vultures and Romulus twelve, the question was decided in favour of Romulus. See Plutarch's *Life of Romulus*.

143. **Let ... five years.** The point here is that Shadwell is taunted with having taken five years to write a play which he pretended he had been obliged to hurry out. In the Prologue to the *Virtuoso* he complains that authors cannot do justice to themselves because they have no time—

" Now drudges of the stage must oft appear,
They must be bound to scribble twice a year."

145. **gentle George**, Sir George Etherege, the wit, poet, and dramatist, author of *The Comical Revenge ; or, Love in a Tub, She Would if She Could*, and *The Man of Mode, or, Sir Fopling Flutter*—all his plays were very successful. He died in 1691.

146, 7. **Dorimant ... Loveit ... Cully, Cockwood, Fopling.** Dorimant, Loveit, and Fopling are characters in Etherege's *Sir*

Foppling Flutter. Cully and Cockwood figure in his *Love in a Tub.*

157. **alien Sedley,** Sir Charles Sedley, the profligate but accomplished wit, dramatist, and minor poet, was intimately acquainted with Dryden, who introduces him as one of the interlocutors in the *Essay of Dramatic Poesy.* Sir Charles had written the Prologue to Shadwell's play, *Epsom Wells,* and in 1679 Shadwell dedicated to Sedley his *True Widow,* in which he thanks him for his assistance in correction and alteration. This was not the first time that charges of plagiarism had been brought against Shadwell. In the Dedication of *Psyche* to the Duke of Monmouth nearly eight years previously he had said, " I have met with some enemies who are always ready to do me the irreparable injury to blast my reputation with the King, and when I have the honour to please him . . . endeavour to persuade him that I do not write the plays I own, or at least that the best part of theuf are written for me." Shadwell's plagiarisms were notorious. " I cannot wholly acquit our present laureate," says his friend Langbaine, "from borrowing; his plagiarisms being in some places too bold and open to be disguised " (*Dramatic Poets,* p. 443). With what stinging force Dryden's accusations must have come home will therefore be obvious.

162. **Sir Formal's oratory.** Sir Formal is ' the orator, a florid coxcomb,' in Shadwell's *Virtuoso,* and his language is in accordance with his character—he is a stilted fool.

164. **northern dedications.** Shadwell dedicates no fewer than six of his plays to the Duke of Newcastle and his family—four to the Duke himself, one to the Duchess, and one to Lord Ogle, the Duke's son, and they certainly are very much in the style of Sir Formal. In the *Vindication of the Duke of Guise,* Dryden refers again to Shadwell as the northern dedicator, if Scott be not correct in reading dictator.

166. **arrogating Jonson's hostile name.** Shadwell is always declaring himself a humble disciple of Ben Jonson, whom, in the preface to *The Virtuoso,* he calls " incomparably the best dramatic poet that ever was, or, I believe, ever will be," adding, " I had rather be author of one scene in his comedies than of any play that this age has produced." See, too, his remarks in the Prefaces to *The Sullen Lovers* and *The Royal Shepherdess,* and particularly the Epilogue to *The Humourists,* where he says—

> " But to out-go all other men would be,
> O noble Ben, less than to follow thee."

173. **Prince Nicander's vein,** an allusion to the scene between Prince Nicander and Psyche, in the first act of Shadwell's *Psyche.*

180. **New humours.** A reference to a passage in the Dedication

of *The Virtuoso.* "Four of the Humours are entirely new, and (without vanity) I may say I ne'er produced a comedy that had not some natural humour in it not represented before, and I hope I never shall."

181. **This is that boasted.** These lines are a parody of four lines in Shadwell's Epilogue to *The Humourists*

"A humour is the bias of the mind
By which with violence 'tis inclin'd,
It makes our actions lean on one side still,
And in all changes that way bend the will."

187. **A tun of man.** See Second Part of *Absalom and Achitophel*, character of Og, where Shadwell is described as "goodly and *great*," a 'monstrous mass,' a 'tun of midnight work' etc.

194. **thy Irish pen.** The imputation of being an Irishman appears to have distressed Shadwell more than anything else in the Satire. "He" (Dryden) "knows that I never saw Ireland till I was three-and-twenty years old, and was there but four months," was poor Shadwell's rejoinder. See Malone, *Life of Dryden*, p. 173.

196-9. **mild anagram ... wings display.** The fashionable poets between the end of Elizabeth's reign and Dryden's time were fond of amusing themselves with these inanities. For an account of them, see D'Israeli's *Curiosities of Literature*, article on "Literary Follies," and Addison's paper on "False Wit," *Spectator*, Number 63. Verses were arrayed in forms of wings, altars, gloves, eggs, and the like. Butler ridicules these amusements in his "Character of a Small Poet" (*Remains*, vol. ii. pp. 118-20). An anagram (Greek, ἀνά, back, again, and γράμμα, a letter or written character) is a change in a word from a transposition of letters, as Juno transformed into Unio. An acrostic is a short poem in which the initial letters of the lines spell a word, from the Greek ἄκρος, point or on the edge, so first, and στίχιον, the diminutive of στίχος, a row, order, or line.

204. **Bruce and Longville ... trap prepared.** A pertinent and amusing allusion to the scene in Shadwell's *Virtuoso* (Act iii.) where Miranda and Clarinda at the instigation of Bruce and Longville abruptly cut short Sir Formal Trifle's speechifying by making him disappear through a trap-door. In the last couplet the reference of course is to the mantle of Elijah falling on Elisha (ii. *Kings*, ii. 13, 4).

INDEX TO NOTES.

The numbers refer to the page on which the note is to be found.

GLASGOW : PRINTED AT THE UNIVERSITY PRESS BY ROBERT MACLEHOSE AND CO. LTD.

DITED WITH INTRODUCTION AND NOTES.

ADDISON—SELECTIONS FROM THE SPECTATOR. By K. Deighton. 2s. 6d.

——THE SPECTATOR. (Essays I.-L.) By Rev. J. Morrison, M.A., D.D. 2s. 6d.

ADDISON and STEELE—COVERLEY PAPERS FROM THE SPECTATOR. By K. Deighton. 1s. 9d.

ARNOLD—SELECTIONS FROM POEMS. By G. C. Macaulay. 2s. 6d.

AYTOUN'S LAYS—By H. B. Cotterill, M.A. 6d.

BACON—ESSAYS. By F. G. Selby, M.A. 3s.

——SELECTIONS FROM BACON'S ESSAYS. First Series. By R. O. Platt. 6d.

——SELECTIONS FROM BACON'S ESSAYS. Second Series. By R. O. Platt. 1s.

——THE ADVANCEMENT OF LEARNING. By F. G. Selby, M.A. Book I., 2s. Book II., 4s. 6d.

——THE NEW ATLANTIS. By A. T. Flux. Sewed, 1s.

BOSWELL—JOURNAL OF A TOUR TO THE HEBRIDES. By H. B. Cotterill, M.A. 2s. 6d.

BUNYAN—PILGRIM'S PROGRESS. By Rev. J. Morrison, M.A., D.D. 1s. 9d.

BURKE—REFLECTIONS ON THE FRENCH REVOLUTION. By F. G. Selby, M.A. 5s.

——SPEECH ON AMERICAN TAXATION; SPEECH ON CONCILIATION WITH AMERICA; LETTER TO THE SHERIFFS OF BRISTOL. By F. G. Selby, M.A. 3s. 6d.

——THOUGHTS ON THE CAUSE OF THE PRESENT DISCONTENTS. By F. G. Selby, M.A. 2s. 6d.

BYRON—CHILDE HAROLD. By Edward E. Morris, M.A. Cantos I. and II., 1s. 9d.; Cantos III. and IV., 1s. 9d.

CAMPBELL—SELECTIONS. By W. T. Webb, M.A. 2s.

CHAUCER—SELECTIONS FROM CANTERBURY TALES. By H. Corson. 4s. 6d.

——THE SQUIRE'S TALE. By A. W. Pollard, M.A. 1s. 6d.

——THE PROLOGUE. By the same. 1s. 9d.

——THE KNIGHT'S TALE. By the same. 1s. 9d.

——THE NUN'S PRIEST'S TALE. By the same. 1s. 6d. ·

CHOSEN ENGLISH—Selections from Wordsworth, Byron, Shelley, Lamb, and Scott. By A. Ellis, B.A. 2s. 6d.

COLERIDGE—THE ANCIENT MARINER. By P. T. Creswell, M.A. 1s.

COWPER—THE TASK. Books IV. and V. By W. T. Webb, M.A. Sewed, 1s. each.

——THE TASK. Book V. Sewed, 6d.

——SELECTIONS FROM LETTERS. By W. T. Webb, M.A. 2s. 6d.

——SHORTER POEMS. By W. T. Webb, M.A. 2s. 6d.

——THE EXPOSTULATION. Sewed. 1s.

DRYDEN—SELECT SATIRES—ABSALOM AND ACHITOPHEL; THE MEDAL; MAC FLECKNOE. By J. Churton Collins, M.A. 1s. 9d.

——THE HIND AND THE PANTHER. By Prof. W. H. Williams. 2s. 6d.

ENGLISH POETRY—FROM BLAKE TO ARNOLD. (1783-1853.) Introduction by C. J. Brennan, M.A. Edited by J. P. Pickburn and J. le Gay Brereton. 2s. 6d.

GOLDSMITH—THE TRAVELLER and THE DESERTED VILLAGE. By A. Barrett, B.A. 1s. 9d. THE TRAVELLER and THE DESERTED VILLAGE, separately, 1s. each, sewed.

——THE TRAVELLER and THE DESERTED VILLAGE. By Prof. J. W. Hales. 6d.

——VICAR OF WAKEFIELD. By Michael Macmillan, D.Litt. 2s. 6d.

GRAY—POEMS. By John Bradshaw, LL.D. 1s. 9d.

——ODE ON SPRING and THE BARD. Sewed, 6d.

——ELEGY IN A COUNTRY CHURCHYARD. Sewed, 6d.

——SELECT ODES. Sewed. 6d.

——LIFE. By Matthew Arnold. Sewed. 6d.

HELPS—ESSAYS WRITTEN IN THE INTERVALS OF BUSINESS. By F. J. Rowe, M.A. and W. T. Webb, M.A. 1s. 9d.

HOLMES—THE AUTOCRAT OF THE BREAKFAST TABLE. By J. Downie, M.A. 2s. 6d.

JOHNSON—LIFE OF MILTON. By K. Deighton. 1s. 9d.

——LIFE OF DRYDEN. By P. Peterson. 2s. 6d.

——LIFE OF POPE. By P. Peterson. 2s. 6d.

LAMB—THE ESSAYS OF ELIA. First Series. By N. L. Hallward, M.A., and S. C. Hill, B.A. 3s. Second Series, 3s.

——TALES FROM SHAKESPEARE. By C. D. Punchard, B.A. 1s. 6d.

LONGFELLOW—COURTSHIP OF MILES STANDISH. By W. Elliot, M.A. 1s.

——THE SONG OF HIAWATHA. By H. B. Cotterill, M.A. 1s. 6d.

——EVANGELINE. By H. B. Cotterill, M.A. 1s. 9d.

MACAULAY—LAYS OF ANCIENT ROME. By W. T. Webb, M.A. 1s. 9d.—HORATIUS, separately, 6d.—ESSAY ON ADDISON. By R. F. Winch, M.A. 2s. 6d.—ESSAY ON WARREN HASTINGS. By K. Deighton. 2s. 6d.—ESSAY ON LORD CLIVE. By K. Deighton. 2s.—ESSAY ON BOSWELL'S LIFE OF JOHNSON. By R. F. Winch, M.A. 2s. 6d.—ESSAY ON WILLIAM PITT, EARL OF CHATHAM. By R. F. Winch, M.A. 2s. 6d.—ESSAY ON MILTON. By H. B. Cotterill, M.A. 2s. 6d.—ESSAY ON FREDERIC THE GREAT. By A. T. Flux. 1s. 9d.—LIFE OF SAMUEL JOHNSON. By H. B. Cotterill, M.A. 2s.—LIFE OF OLIVER GOLDSMITH. By the same. 2s.—LIFE OF PITT. By R. E. Winch, M.A. 2s.

MALORY— MORTE D'ARTHUR. By A. T. Martin, M.A. 2s. 6d.

MILTON—PARADISE LOST. Books I. and II. By Michael Macmillan, D.Litt.
1s. 9d. Books I.-IV., separately, 1s 3d. each; Book III., sewed, 1s.—LYCIDAS
SONNETS, &c. By W. Bell, M.A. 1s. 9d.—PARADISE LOST. Book VI. By H.
B. Cotterill, M.A. 1s.—AREOPAGITICA. By the same. 2s.—COMUS. By W. Bell,
M.A. 1s. 3d.—LYCIDAS. By the same. Sewed, 6d.—SAMSON AGONISTES. By
H. M. Percival, M.A. 2s.—TRACTATE OF EDUCATION. By E. E Morris, M.A.
1s. 9d.—LYCIDAS AND COMUS. By W. Bell, M.A. 1s. 6d.

MORE.—THE UTOPIA OF SIR THOMAS MORE. By H. B. Cotterill, M.A. 2s. 6d.

PALGRAVE—GOLDEN TREASURY OF SONGS AND LYRICS. Book I. By J. H. Fowler,
M.A. 1s. 6d. Book II. By W. Bell, M.A. 1s. 6d. Book III. By J. H. Fowler.
1s. 6d. Book IV. Edited by J.H. Fowler. 1s. 6d. Notes to Books I. to IV. 2s. 6d.

POEMS OF ENGLAND. A Selection of English Patriotic Poetry. By Here-
ford B. George, M.A., and Arthur Sidgwick, M.A. 2s. 6d.

POPE—ESSAY ON MAN. Epistles I.-IV. By E. E. Morris M.A. 1s. 3d.; sewed, 1s.
—— ESSAY ON MAN. Epistle I. Sewed, 6d.
—— ESSAY ON CRITICISM. By J. C. Collins, M.A. 1s. 9d.

REPRESENTATIVE ENGLISH POEMS. By G. S. BRETT. 3s. 6d.

SCOTT—THE LADY OF THE LAKE. By G. H. Stuart, M.A. 2s. 6d.; Canto I.,
sewed, 9d.—THE LAY OF THE LAST MINSTREL. By G. H. Stuart, M.A., and E. H.
Elliot, B.A. 2s. Canto I., sewed, 9d. Cantos I.-III., 1s. 3d.; sewed, 1s
MARMION. By Michael Macmillan, D.Litt. 3s. Cantos I. and VI., 1s. Canto
VI., 1s.—ROKEBY. By the same. 3s.—THE LORD OF THE ISLES. By H. B.
Cotterill, M.A. 2s. 6d.—QUENTIN DURWARD. 2s. 6d.—KENILWORTH. 2s. 6d.
—THE TALISMAN. 2s. 6d.—WOODSTOCK. 2s. 6d.—FORTUNES OF NIGEL. 2s. 6d.
—IVANHOE. 2s. 6d.—OLD MORTALITY. 2s. 6d.

SELECTED POEMS from Gray, Burns, Cowper, Moore, Longfellow. By H. B.
Cotterill, M.A. 1s.

SHAKESPEARE—Plays edited by K. Deighton.—THE TEMPEST, 1s. 9d. MUCH
ADO ABOUT NOTHING, 2s. A MIDSUMMER NIGHT'S DREAM, 1s. 9d. THE MERCHANT
OF VENICE, 1s. 9d. AS YOU LIKE IT, 1s. 9d. TWELFTH NIGHT, 1s. 9d. THE
WINTER'S TALE, 2s. KING JOHN, 1s. 9d. RICHARD II., 1s. 9d. HENRY IV.,
Part I., 2s. 6d. HENRY IV., Part II., 2s. 6d. HENRY V., 1s. 9d. HENRY VIII.,
1s. 9d. CORIOLANUS, 2s. 6d.; sewed, 2s. ROMEO AND JULIET, 2s. 6d. JULIUS
CÆSAR, 1s. 9d. MACBETH, 1s. 9d. HAMLET, 2s. 6d.; sewed, 2s. KING LEAR,
1s. 9d. OTHELLO, 2s. 6d. ANTONY AND CLEOPATRA, 2s. 6d.; sewed, 2s. CYMBELINE,
2s. 6d. TWO GENTLEMEN OF VERONA, 1s. 9d.
——RICHARD III., by C. H. Tawney, M.A. 2s. 6d.

SOUTHEY—LIFE OF NELSON. By Michael Macmillan, D.Litt. 3s.

SPENSER—THE FAERIE QUEENE. Book I. By H. M. Percival, M.A. 3s.
——THE SHEPHEARDS CALENDAR. By C. H. Herford, Litt.D. 2s. 6d.

STEELE—SELECTIONS. By L. E. Steele, M.A. 2s.

TENNYSON—SELECTIONS. By F. J. Rowe, M.A., and W. T. Webb, M.A. 3s. 6d.
Also in two parts, 2s. 6d. each. Part I. Recollections of the Arabian Nights,
The Lady of Shalott, The Lotos-Eaters, Dora, Ulysses, Tithonus, The Lord of
Burleigh, The Brook, Ode on the Death of the Duke of Wellington, The Re-
venge.—Part II. Œnone, The Palace of Art, A Dream of Fair Women, Morte
D'Arthur, Sir Galahad, The Voyage, Demeter and Persephone.
—THE LOTOS-EATERS, ULYSSES, ODE ON THE DUKE OF WELLINGTON, MAUD,
COMING OF ARTHUR AND PASSING OF ARTHUR. By the same. 2s. 6d.
——COMING AND PASSING OF ARTHUR, DREAM OF FAIR WOMEN, THE LOTOS-EATERS,
ULYSSES, ODE ON THE DUKE OF WELLINGTON, THE REVENGE. By the same. 3s. 6d.
——MORTE D'ARTHUR. By the same, sewed 1s.
——THE COMING OF ARTHUR; THE PASSING OF ARTHUR. By F. J. Rowe, M.A. 2s. 6d.
——ENOCH ARDEN. By W. T. Webb, M.A. 2s. 6d.
——AYLMER'S FIELD. By W. T. Webb, M.A. 2s. 6d.
——THE PRINCESS. By Percy M. Wallace, M.A. 3s. 6d.
——GARETH AND LYNETTE. By G. C. Macaulay, M.A. 2s. 6d.
——GERAINT AND ENID; THE MARRIAGE OF GERAINT. By the same. 2s 6d.
——THE HOLY GRAIL. By the same. 2s. 6d.
——LANCELOT AND ELAINE. By F. J. Rowe, M.A 2s. 6d.
——GUINEVERE. By G. C. Macaulay, M.A. 2s 6d.
——SELECT POEMS OF TENNYSON. By H. B. George and W. H. Hadow. 2s. 6d.
——THE CUP. By H. B. Cotterill, M.A. 2s. 6d.
——TIRESIAS AND OTHER POEMS. By F. J. Rowe, M.A., and W. T. Webb, M.A. 2s. 6d.
——IN MEMORIAM. By H. M. Percival, M.A. 2s. 6d.

THACKERAY—Esmond. 2s. 6d.

WORDSWORTH—SELECTIONS. By W. T. Webb, M.A. 2s. 6d. Also in two

Lightning Source UK Ltd.
Milton Keynes UK
UKOW06f1819210116

266845UK00022B/984/P

9 781330 974018